Byrd's Line

❋ BYRD'S LINE

A Natural History

STEPHEN CONRAD AUSBAND

WITHDRAWN

University of Virginia Press • Charlottesville and London

University of Virginia Press

© 2002 by the Rector and Visitors of the University of Virginia

All rights reserved

Printed in the United States of America on acid-free paper

First published 2002

9 8 7 6 5 4 3 2 1

Excerpts from William Byrd's work are reprinted by permission of the pub-
lisher from *The Prose Works of William Byrd of Westover,* edited by Louis B. Wright. Cambridge, Mass.: The Belknap Press of Harvard University Press. Copyright © 1966 by the
President and Fellows of Harvard College.

LIBRARY OF CONGRESS CATALOGING-IN-PUBLICATION DATA

Ausband, Stephen C., 1943–

    Byrd's line : a natural history / Stephen Conrad Ausband.

        p.   cm.

    Includes bibliographical references (p.   ).

    ISBN 0-8139-2134-1 (cloth : alk. paper)—ISBN 0-8139-2135-X
    (pbk. : alk. paper)

    1. Virginia—Description and travel. 2. North Carolina—Description and
    travel. 3. Virginia—Boundaries—North Carolina. 4. North Carolina—
    Boundaries—Virginia. 5. Byrd, William, 1674–1744—Journeys—Virginia.
    6. Byrd, William, 1674–1744—Journeys—North Carolina. 7. Natural history—
    Virginia. 8. Natural history—North Carolina. 9. Virginia—Surveys.
    10. North Carolina—Surveys. I. Title.

    F229 .A88 2002

    508.755—dc21

                                                    2002003117

Contents

Preface and Acknowledgments

IT HAS BEEN nearly 275 years since William Byrd of Westover, along with other commissioners and surveyors and woodsmen from North Carolina and Virginia, defined the line separating those two colonies. It has been more than 30 years since I first discovered the witty, elegant, erudite prose in which Byrd wrote his two accounts of the task. I remember wondering then what kind of man this must have been, to have been so headstrong and opinionated and yet so accurate and careful in his observations of the world around him.

Perhaps the best words to describe Byrd are "curious" and "vain." He wanted to know everything, to touch everything, and even to talk about everything, and he wanted to see himself doing all this in the mirror of his own writing. To this end he kept secret diaries recording, matter-of-factly, his day-to-day business dealings, his acquisition of more and more land, his observations of natural phenomena, his sexual ardor for other women (married or not, to his friends or not), his regimen of daily calisthenics (which he called his dance), his private religious devotions, his almost daily reading of ancient texts, and even his lovemaking with his wife.

Byrd's two accounts of the dividing line between Virginia and North Carolina are important as literary and historical documents. Scholars study them because of the insight they give us into the mind and art of a man who—in his own mind, but not only in his own mind—represented much that was typical of a well-educated, sophisticated Englishman in the New World during the early eighteenth century. The accounts are also important, however, as natural histories. They give us insight into the natural world just as it was being touched—and irrevocably changed—by the Europeans.

I have chosen to call this book a natural history even though I am no more a professional scientist than William Byrd was. I have hunted, fished, explored, and tramped around in most of the territory Byrd traversed in 1728, taking notes and photographs, and the book might therefore be seen as a kind of dialogue between two men with similar interests, looking at the same piece of territory but separated by almost three hundred years. Neither this book nor Byrd's *History of the Dividing Line* was written specifically for scientists. Rather, my intended audience is the man or woman one early reviewer of the manuscript called "Samuel Johnson's 'Common Reader'"—a term I find attractive and precise, and one I am sure Byrd would have approved as well. Those "Common Readers" with an interest in plants and animals, ecology, colonial American history, and American literature will, I hope, find something of interest in the following pages.

In his day William Byrd was fond of imagining what the land he saw could become in the future. Sometimes now we must look back and imagine what the land we see has been in the past. There is a continuity in our looking back, as we see more clearly what has changed and what has remained the same. My hope is that this book will provide an interesting place to stand as we look.

I am grateful to The Belknap Press of Harvard University Press for granting permission to quote from Louis B. Wright's edition of *The Prose Works of William Byrd of Westover*. I want to thank Edward Fisher and William Hathaway, both of the Department of Biology at Averett University, for their help in identifying the various plant species discussed in the book. Bill Hathaway's encyclopedic knowledge of plant distribution in Virginia and of the common names of plants (current and antique) was especially helpful. I would also like to thank J. I. Hayes, our American history specialist (whose office is so conveniently located that I could bother him at will), and Boyd Zenner, my acquisitions editor at the University of Virginia Press, whose patient advice on and confidence in the manuscript at various stages of preparation were very helpful. Finally, I would like to thank Ann Garbett, Beth Tucker, Carol Barton, and Melinda Ausband for proofreading and correcting parts of the manuscript. Any errors that remain are entirely my own.

Byrd's Line

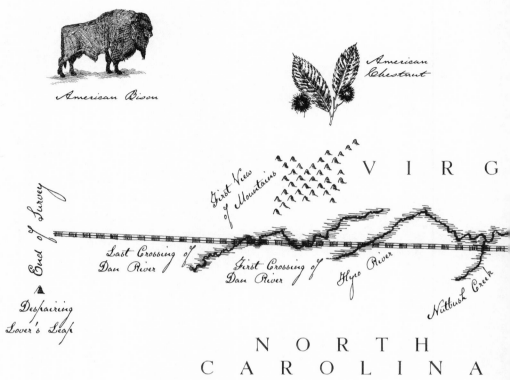

American Bison

American Chestnut

End of Survey

First View of Mountains

V I R G

Last Crossing of Dan River

First Crossing of Dan River

Hyco River

Nutbush Creek

Despairing Lover's Leap

N O R T H

C A R O L I N A

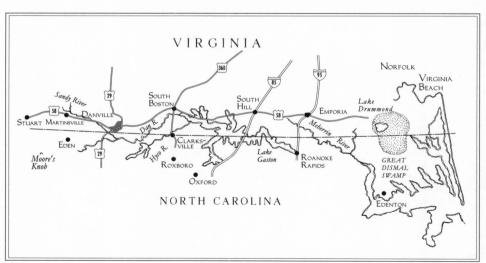

VIRGINIA

360

85

95

NORFOLK

VIRGINIA BEACH

Sandy River

29

SOUTH BOSTON

SOUTH HILL

EMPORIA

Lake Drummond

STUART MARTINSVILLE

58

DANVILLE

Dan R.

CLARKS-VILLE

58

Mcherrin River

Moore's Knob

29

EDEN

Hyco R.

ROXBORO

Lake Gaston

ROANOKE RAPIDS

GREAT DISMAL SWAMP

OXFORD

EDENTON

NORTH CAROLINA

Mountain Lion

Flowering Dogwood

Snakeweed

I N I A

First Crossing
of Roanoke

Meherrin River

Blackwater
(Weyanoke Creek)

Nottoway
Creek

Somerton

Great
Dismal
Swamp

Currituck Inlet
(Beginning)

Great Falls
of Roanoke

Edenton

N

W   E

S

White Oak

Red Wolf

0   Miles   25

Abbreviations

H   Byrd, William. *The History of the Dividing Line betwixt Virginia and North Carolina. Run in the Year of Our Lord 1728.* In *The Prose Works of William Byrd of Westover,* edited by Louis B. Wright, 157–336. Cambridge: The Belknap Press of Harvard University Press, 1966.

SH Byrd, William. *The Secret History of the Line.* In *The Prose Works of William Byrd of Westover,* edited by Louis B. Wright, 41–153. Cambridge: The Belknap Press of Harvard University Press, 1966.

✳ INTRODUCTION

Who Was Byrd and What Was the Dividing Line?

WILLIAM BYRD II was born in eastern Virginia in the spring of 1674. Like many children of wealthy planter parents at the time, he was sent to England to be educated, leaving Virginia at the age of seven and not returning until 1696, at the age of twenty-two. His schooling (at Felsted Grammar School, in Essex) gave him a solid background in the classics and, apparently, a lifelong love of learning, for his Virginia diaries much later record his almost daily reading in Latin, Greek, and Hebrew and his interest in translating the classics. He acquired skill in business by working for the merchant house of Perry and Lane, then he entered the Middle Temple in 1692 to study law.

As a student of law, an educated gentleman, and a handsome, witty young man, Byrd became a bon vivant. He attended plays, met the playwrights Congreve and Wycherley, and tried his hand at poetry and translation. Though not a scientist himself, Byrd had a keen interest in natural science, and he numbered among his friends and associates many genuine men of science, some of whom were very influential. The result was that he was elected to membership in the Royal Society in 1696, just a few months before he was to return to Virginia.

On returning home to manage his father's estates, the young lawyer and urbanite demonstrated a shrewd head for business and a passion for the acquisition of more land. The estate of the senior Byrd was already large, but by the time William Byrd II had finished adding to it, the family holdings were immense. Before his death in 1744, his property amounted to over 180,000 acres (over 280 square miles) in North Carolina and Virginia. Byrd's father had not only been a successful plantation owner; he had also set up trade with the Indians, and his traders traveled hundreds of miles into North and South Carolina, visiting the Cherokees and Catawbas. His son would carry on the Indian trade and become a minor political figure in the new colony, but his major business would remain agriculture, and he never tired of acquiring land. As Pierre Marambaud has pointed out, the growing of tobacco as a principal crop wore out land very quickly, and so land-owners were constantly in need of more acreage (158).

Byrd built a house, Westover, which is now regarded as one of the finest examples of Georgian architecture in the United States. He collected paintings and books, encouraged the flourishing of the arts in the colony, and made his library one of the best in all of Virginia in the early eighteenth century. During all this time Byrd was also cultivating an eye for detail, a witty prose style, and a keen interest in the flora, the fauna, and the native human inhabitants of the New World.

In the spring and fall of 1728, Byrd led a surveying party charged with the important task of determining the exact boundary between Virginia and North Carolina. His account of the survey, *The History of the Dividing Line betwixt Virginia and North Carolina, Run in the Year of Our Lord 1728,* has become a minor classic of colonial American literature. Another account, *The Secret History of the Line,* describes the same events and places but more lightheartedly—and frequently more scandalously—using pseudonyms and devoting more attention to personality conflicts and personal vices among the surveyors. He published neither account during his lifetime, preferring to circulate them among friends in the fashion of an erudite gentleman for whom excellent and interesting writing was simply one more social grace.

There are distinct differences in tone and style between the two accounts, which may be accounted for by considering Byrd's purpose in writing them. Both were consciously literary works drawing on his notes and on a fairly straightforward account of the expedition that he presented to the Crown a short time after the survey had been completed. *The Secret History,* which was written first, is witty and satirical and very much in the fashion of a clever urbanite looking with be-mused (and occasionally outraged) interest on the foolishness of his country cousins, especially the ones from North Carolina. In an age of satire, Byrd wanted to be a good satirist.

The History is much longer and much more digressive. Byrd worked on it at intervals, apparently, for ten years after the actual survey, again drawing on his notes and reworking the account he had written ear-lier in *The Secret History*. In *The History* Byrd not only describes the land and the plant and animal life but also makes learned sounding comparisons between what he discovers along the line and what might be seen in Africa, say, or in Greenland or South America. It is probable that the later account was intended for an audience that would include scientists, amateur enthusiasts of the natural sciences, and learned gentlemen. His friends back in London, including those in the Royal Academy, must have been uppermost in his mind.

There were pressing reasons why an accurate line had to be drawn, not the least of which was the desire of the government of Virginia to collect taxes from people living along its southern borders and claim-ing to be residents of North Carolina (where, according to Byrd, there were neither tax collectors nor any other representatives of a standing government, the land being mostly wilderness and the people nearly as wild as the land). Accordingly, Byrd's party of Virginians met with a party of Carolina surveyors in March, 1728, on the north shore of Currituck Inlet, and their very first joint activity was to quarrel about exactly where to begin drawing the line.

Early charters differed in their accounts of where the line be-tween North Carolina and Virginia should be drawn. A grant from King Charles II to the earl of Clarendon and others, dated 24 March 1663, set a boundary along "a due-west line from . . . Colleton Island, lying in 36 degrees of north latitude, quite to the South Sea" (*H* 168). Two years later, a second grant extended the North Carolina lands a little over thirty miles northward, declaring the line to run "from the north end of Currituck Inlet due west to Weyanoke Creek, lying within or about the degree of thirty-six and thirty minutes of north-ern latitude, and from thence west in a direct line as far as the South

Sea" (*H* 169). Another survey, one done by that indefatigable amateur naturalist and surveyor John Lawson in 1710, also fixed the line at 36°30′ N.

One major problem in determining the exact location was that Currituck Inlet, like all inlets along the thin barrier islands, was constantly shifting its position and was, in fact, partly filled in by the second decade of the eighteenth century. A second and perhaps more serious problem was that Weyanoke Creek had been lost; no one could agree on which stream the name might originally have designated, and the difference between possible candidates amounted to several miles.

After some argument and compromise, Byrd's party agreed to begin the line at a point of high ground on the north shore of Currituck Inlet, the high ground being chosen since the flat sand to the south of it was more obviously subject to the vagaries of tide and current. This put the easternmost portion of the line, according to Byrd's instruments, at 36°31′ N. About fifty-five miles to the west of the beginning point, just above where the Blackwater River flows into the Nottoway River, Byrd determined that he had found what must be Weyanoke Creek. At this point he dropped the line a few hundred yards south, to the mouth of the Blackwater, at 36°30′ N, and continued his survey on a due west track. This accounts for the small dogleg in the current line between the two states, for subsequent mapmakers generally followed Byrd's lead, even if they did not always follow his exact survey line or agree with his measurements. Today's boundary between the two states is closer to 36°33′ N (in its easternmost portion), but where Gates and Hertford Counties in North Carolina come together with Suffolk and Southampton Counties in Virginia, the line still runs exactly north-south for a half mile.

Byrd's line stretched approximately 241 miles. (His own accounts of the distance vary, but the figure 241 seems about right.) It ended just south of what is now Stuart, Virginia, and within sight of what Byrd described as "prodigiously high" mountains: "Their distance seemed to be no more than five or six miles" (*SH* 128).

It is important for the modern reader to understand that while much of Virginia along the James, the York, and the Rappahannock

Rivers was settled territory in the early eighteenth century, with large plantations and thriving little communities such as Norfolk, Williamsburg, and Jamestown, the area along the survey line was largely without white settlers. Byrd's party had considerable difficulty even finding someone who could tell them how to get from Norfolk to Currituck Inlet. The survey line crossed several large farms on Knott's Island and on either side of the Great Dismal Swamp, but by the time the surveyors reached the Meherrin River, in April 1728, they were almost completely beyond all farms and settlements. The last large farm was one owned by a Colonel Mumford, "on the south side of Roanoke," about twenty miles north and west of the present town of Roanoke Rapids, North Carolina. By the time the surveyors had reached the Hyco River, near the present town of Clarksville, Virginia, they determined that they had left the last white inhabitants fifty miles behind them.

Byrd recorded every interesting geographical feature, watercourse, and physical obstacle the party encountered. He described the plant and animal life accurately and in great detail: the towering chestnut trees (once the dominant arboreal species, along with oak and hickory, in these southeastern forests but now vanished), the maidenhair fern (for which he claimed "excellent pectoral virtues"), and the abundance of game animals and predators. These included not only deer and bear but also buffalo, panthers, and wolves. Among the birds he mentioned are the now-extinct Carolina parakeet and the passenger pigeon, both of which he found much less interesting than the wild turkeys.

About a few natural details Byrd was simply mistaken. He believed, for instance, that the Great Dismal Swamp was almost void of life due to the "foul miasmas" arising from its waters during the summer. He seemed endlessly fascinated by the notion that certain plants were efficacious in the treatment of snakebite. He cites several far-fetched but popular superstitions about reptiles, including the American alligator. For the most part, though, he was reliable, accurate, and graphically informative as he recorded the party's difficulties with swamps, rivers, tangled growth, and rough terrain and as he mused on the fertile land, the abundance of animal life, and the nature of the few red and white inhabitants the group encountered.

Most of the area right along the survey line, especially that portion lying west of the Meherrin River, was still wilderness in 1728, with no towns and few farms; Byrd described it repeatedly as lawless and sparsely settled. For that matter, he tended to regard all of North Carolina as lawless and unsettled. He referred to the colony as "Lubberland" and said it was full of indolent scofflaws who lived by growing a little corn and letting their hogs run wild in the woods to fatten on acorns, only bothering to look for the animals when they needed fresh pork. "Surely," he said, "there is no place in the world where the inhabitants live with less labor than in North Carolina. It approaches nearer to the description of Lubberland than any other, by the great felicity of the climate, the easiness of raising provisions, and the slothfulness of the people. . . . To speak the truth, 'tis a thorough aversion to labor that makes people file off to North Carolina, where plenty and a warm sun confirm them in their disposition to laziness for their whole lives" (*H* 204–5). Byrd's comments were as much motivated by politics as by snobbery, as Marambaud and others have pointed out (122). He was anxious, in a book that might be read abroad, for his own to appear the superior colony. Still, there is a strong element of the settled, successful landowner's antipathy toward the unruly frontiersman and scofflaw in all these comments.

Members of Byrd's party and their counterparts from North Carolina drove a cedar post into the ground near the Atlantic Ocean, just north of Currituck Inlet, on the morning of 7 March 1728 and began the survey. They worked until the end of April, by which time both parties agreed to let the project wait until the fall, when the snakes were not as plentiful and vigorous. They resumed work on 19 September, reaching their westernmost point (about five miles south of the present town of Stuart, on the Patrick County, Virginia/Stokes County, North Carolina line) on the 26th of the following month.

This book retraces William Byrd's journey along the dividing line in order to compare the area as it is now to the land as Byrd described it more than 270 years ago. Small sections of the countryside along the line are remarkably like they were then; most of it, however, has been altered drastically. The Great Dismal Swamp is smaller in total area than it was in 1728, but its status as a National Wildlife Refuge

has helped preserve its integrity. The huge chestnut trees Bryd described are gone from the wooded slopes of piedmont hillsides, replaced by oak-hickory forests, and the nearly unbroken woods have
given way in most places to farmland, towns, and cities. Byrd's dividing line, drawn in 1728 through land that was heavily forested and
sparsely populated, has been cut by roads and spanned by bridges,
paved over or developed as shopping malls and subdivisions, plowed
and farmed, or (in the area now covered by Kerr and Gaston Reservoirs) simply flooded. He dreamed of some of these changes, and he
wrote enthusiastically about the possibility of fertile farms and busy
villages in the vast and promising territory.

Much of the wildlife remains, having been brought back by enlightened wildlife-management practices in the last half century. Deer,
bears, and turkeys flourish along parts of the line, as do most species
of the waterfowl and the smaller game he observed. (See the comments about individual species in the chapters that follow.) The passenger pigeons and Carolina parakeets are gone, as are the buffalo and
panthers. The wolves are back, though—at least fairly close to Byrd's
line. They have been reintroduced successfully on the Alligator River
National Wildlife Refuge, not far south of the line, and their howling
at night sounds just the way Byrd described it.

A modern highway map of Virginia or North Carolina (either will
do, since either will show a few miles of territory beyond its own borders and into the neighboring state) provides an idea of where Byrd's
line is in relation to major highways, towns, and cities. Concentrating
only on that area of the map lying within approximately fifteen miles
north and south of the dividing line, one focuses on exactly the long,
narrow corridor through which Byrd traveled in the eighteenth century. There are, of course, many more roads, towns, and cities marked
on the modern map than there were in the area nearly three hundred
years ago, but at least the map gives an indication of the distances involved in each stage of the survey.

Beginning on 7 March 1728, Byrd and his party worked their way
westward from the Atlantic Ocean toward what now shows on the
map as U.S. 258. The surveyors had to carry a straight line through
swamps, forests, salt marshes, and a few farms as well as over water-

ways. It took them ten days to reach a spot well to the east of where U.S. 17 crosses the line today—a distance of just over twenty miles. By the time they had fought their way through the Great Dismal Swamp and the tangled low grounds beyond it to reach the area roughly where U.S. 258 crosses the line, the date was 2 April. They had been at their work almost a month and had covered a little less than sixty miles. They temporarily abandoned the task three days (and about thirteen miles) later, resolving to come back in the fall, when they were rested, better armed and provisioned for the much longer, more dangerous task to come, and, as Byrd explained, when the rattlesnakes were less active.

They resumed work on 19 September, carrying the line from the point where they had stopped to a place a few miles east of where U.S. 29 now crosses the line just south of Danville, Virginia—a distance of a little over one hundred miles. Carrying the line this far, through swamps and low grounds but, increasingly now, through more open deciduous forests on higher, rolling ground and rocky piedmont soil, took until 10 October. Three days later they had progressed another ten miles, and, the day "being Sunday," Byrd noted, "we rested from our fatigue and had leisure to reflect on the signal mercies of Providence" (*H* 246). In the distance they could see the peaks of mountains.

From this point their journey carried them into the foothills of the Blue Ridge range—"within the shadow of the Cherokee mountains," Byrd said, "where we were obliged to set up our pillars, like Hercules, and return home" (*H* 320). The place where they stopped and turned around is halfway between U.S. 29 and Interstate 77, or a few miles south of what is now Stuart, Virginia. When they finally got home, on 22 November, they had been gone more than two months and had extended the line another 180 miles.

Approximately forty miles north of the line, the town of Norfolk was just beginning to become an important center of trade. Byrd remarked that the place had "most the air of a town of any in Virginia," and he added, "the two cardinal virtues that make a place thrive, industry and frugality, are seen here in perfection; and as long as they can banish luxury and idleness the town will remain in a happy and flourishing condition" (*H* 173). About an equal distance to the south of the line, the little port town of Edenton, on Albemarle Sound, had recently become the colonial capital of North Carolina. These are the only two towns of any size that Byrd mentions during the journey. He refers to farms and plantations (such as Mr. Eyland's, Mr. Merchant's, Colonel Mumford's, Captain Embry's), all of them in the eastern third of the survey line, and he mentions Fort Christanna, well north of the line, and the tiny community at Somerton Chapel, barely in Virginia. He saw no other traces of English civilization on the 241-mile journey.

Comparing the modern map with the text of Byrd's accounts also gives an idea of what the terrain was like in the early eighteenth century. The area on either side of the line was almost without any roads at all (except for the few leading out of Norfolk, and the few connecting plantations with little towns such as Edenton). The woods and swamps from Knott's Island to the Nottoway River were broken only occasionally by cleared fields and pastures or plowed lands where Virginia or Carolina colonists had settled. Byrd found the clearings and farms to be much more widely scattered from the Nottoway to the Meherrin and almost nonexistent from the Meherrin to the Roanoke River. From the Roanoke westward, there were no more farms at all. There were paths, to be sure—trading paths and "the route the northern savages take when they go out to war against the Catawbas and other southern nations" (*H* 257). Some (but by no means all) of the rivers and streams beyond the Roanoke had names. There was no real farmland at all, and the few open areas that remained beyond the river were usually the result of fires started naturally or by the Indians. All the rest was only swamps, thickets, canebrakes, and seemingly endless forests.

This was the world William Byrd saw in 1728, and he described it with interest and enthusiasm. He named unnamed rivers, streams, and mountains; he wondered if buffalo could be domesticated and used as cattle; he elaborated on the feeding habits of panthers and bears; he explained that orchards were difficult to maintain because of the huge flights of parakeets in the summer; and he noted that the passenger pigeons would sometimes roost in such numbers that they would break the limbs of chestnut trees. He cast covetous eyes on the

rich bottomland along the Dan and Roanoke Rivers, probably making plans already to return and claim huge sections of that land as his
own. He provided detailed (and sometimes inaccurate) information
about rattlesnakes, alligators, beavers, and wild turkeys. He concocted
remedies for fever, gout, and indigestion from local plants he found
along the way, and he speculated endlessly about the uses of other
plants, especially those with reputed power to cure snakebite. He worried about possible contact with hostile Indians and wondered about
the sources of rivers he crossed.

The colonies on both sides of the dividing line grew rapidly. In
1720, eight years before the survey, North Carolina's population was
only 36,000 people—about enough to fill what most modern readers
would regard as a good-sized small town. In the same year Virginia's
total population was almost 88,000, or about one-third the number
of people now living in the city of Norfolk. By the time the Revolu-
tionary War broke out the Carolina colony had 345,000 people, while
Virginia's population was pushing the half-million mark. (The current combined population of both states is approximately 15 million
people.)

Still, much of the development and population growth has always
been well to the north and south of the dividing line. The Great Dismal Swamp was never successfully drained and farmed, despite the
dreams of both William Byrd and (a generation later) George Washington that such a project would be feasible. The numerous swamps
and lowlands along the eastern section of the line slowed population
growth there, and the western section became farming country for the
most part (as Byrd had hoped it would), without many cities or in-
dustrial areas of any size.

I chose to begin the book where Byrd began drawing the line
rather than beginning with his discussion of the need for an accurate
boundary, or with his description of the town of Norfolk or the difficulty the explorers had in getting from Norfolk to the place where
they were supposed to begin the survey. In the chapters that follow, I
have selected for comment and explanation all the descriptions in
Byrd's accounts that deal specifically with topography, plant and animal
life, watercourses, or (insofar as they are essential to an understanding

of his journey) his contact with various Indian tribes. William Byrd would have lumped together all these items under the category "natural history," the study of which, in the eighteenth century, was often the province of erudite amateurs rather than professional scientists.

A brief introduction to each of the chapters describes Byrd's location along the survey line, summarizes the experiences of the party along this section of the line, and gives the modern reader a view of how the area appears today. Byrd's descriptions of the "natural history" that he saw in 1728—along with his musings, philosophical speculations, private jokes, and sometimes caustic, sometimes enthusiastic observations—follow the introductory material. My own comments on these items are interspersed among Byrd's in order to present an overall view of the area by observers from two very different centuries. By this recurrent juxtaposition of what he saw, commented on, or speculated about and what I have seen and recorded in the same area, I hope to give the sense of a conversation stretching across three centuries.

My selections from *The History of the Dividing Line* and *The Secret History* include only those entries or partial entries relevant to a study of the natural history of the area. I rely on Louis B. Wright's edition of Byrd's prose works, which modernizes much of Byrd's capitalization, punctuation, and spelling from that in the original manuscripts. I have included scientific names for each species the first time it is discussed and in the index. At other times I use common names, except when I think there might be a possibility of confusing one plant or animal with another, similar one.

1 ✳ SPRINGTIME

Currituck Inlet, the Great Dismal, and Beyond

WHERE IS the best place to begin? I suppose exactly where Byrd began, or at least where he began the actual survey of the line, on a windswept stretch of beach some twenty miles south of the coastal resort city of Virginia Beach and approximately fifty miles north of Nags Head, North Carolina.

It would seem to be an easy drive from either of these popular resort areas, and it would be easy except for one thing: there are no paved roads leading to this place, or even very close to it. To reach this point, one has to drive south out of Virginia Beach until the road ends at Back Bay National Wildlife Refuge. From there one can walk or ride a bike (the only wheeled transportation allowed) along the trails leading through False Cape State Park. The bike trails themselves stop about five miles from the point of Byrd's beginning. From there, one has to hike straight down the beach. Alternatively, one can drive northward along the beach in a four-wheel-drive vehicle from Corolla, near the northernmost lighthouse in North Carolina, at the edge of the Currituck National Wildlife Refuge. A small beach community (Corova Beach) exists at the extreme northern tip of the peninsula, approximately ten miles from the paved road. Homeowners and a few vacation renters drive the beach at low tide to get to the houses, as vehicular traffic through the refuge itself is not allowed. No vehicles at all are permitted on the Virginia side of the line.

The area seems remote today—or at least it does after one leaves the crowded beaches, with their throngs of tourists in shorts and suntan oil, and the boys hanging out with surfboards near their four-wheel-drive vehicles, socializing and waiting for the surf to build. In 1728 it was so remote that Byrd did not know exactly how to get there. He searched for a guide to the inlet until he finally got, at least, a set of directions: "There was no soul in the town [Norfolk] knew how the land lay betwixt this place and Currituck Inlet, till at last Mr. William Wilkins, that lives upon the borders, drew a rough sketch that gave a general notion of it. The light given by this draft determined the commissioners to march to the landing of Northwest River and there embark in a piragua in order to meet the commissioners of Carolina at Currituck" (*SH* 51–52).

The maritime forest in False Cape State Park is pristine, a rare find along the popular southeastern coast, and the Commonwealth of Virginia intends to keep it that way. There are low, thick forests of oak, cedar, and yaupon—all species observed by Byrd—and the wildlife in the area still includes the wild hogs he mentioned. The hogs are feral swine that, having escaped their owners generations ago, are as wild as the deer with which they share this barrier strand. Wild horses, common today in the Currituck Wildlife Management Area south of the line, do not appear in Byrd's accounts.

The only venomous snake in the park is the cottonmouth water moccasin, which seems almost ubiquitous in the brackish pools on the back side of the island. Byrd, who was particularly fascinated by rattlesnakes, snakebites, and home remedies for snakebites, does not even mention the very common and sometimes belligerent cottonmouth.

Byrd's line begins at what was once the north shore of an inlet, Currituck Inlet, which was already shoaling in and closing in the early eighteenth century. There is no trace of it at all today. To reach the site his group left Norfolk on foot, sailed down the Northwest River to its entrance into Albemarle Sound, and sailed around Knott's Island to the barrier islands. After some debate with the North Carolina commissioners, Byrd's party agreed to start the line at a high point of land on the north side of the inlet, and they drove a cedar post deeply into the sand to mark the spot. They recorded their position as 36°31′ N latitude.

It took the two parties of surveyors a little over a week to cut a line from the inlet across Knott's Island and through the mainland swamps and forests between the ocean and the Dismal Swamp. On the way Byrd described useful plants (such as silk grass), great stands of trees hung with Spanish moss, and thickets so full of reeds and briars that no breeze could penetrate them. He commented on yaupon bushes and bayberry trees, and he offered his opinions on a hermit and a family of escaped slaves. All the while he seemed to be dreading the encounter he knew was coming, when the group must cut the line through the Dismal Swamp itself.

Byrd did not actually penetrate the swamp. He and the rest of the commissioners from both states retreated southward to the little town of Edenton, on Albemarle Sound, while a small party of adventurous surveyors, including his friend William Mayo, hacked its way through the Dismal. Most of Byrd's comments about natural history in this section concern the plants and animals just south and west of the great swamp. Most of his other comments are fairly scurrilous ones about the residents of Edenton in particular and North Carolina in general.

It seems particularly odd that Byrd, avid naturalist that he was, so easily dismissed the Great Dismal as an empty wasteland. He could be fascinated by the idea of untrammeled wilderness far to the west of the great swamp, and he waxed almost poetic about the virgin forests along the Dan River valley, but he remained steadfast in his notion that there was simply nothing of interest in the Dismal. The noxious vapors supposed to rise from the spongy ground, the unwholesome damps, the lack of light because of the thickly interlaced vegetation, all seemed to Byrd to rule out the possibility of any abundance of life. The whole place was, in his eighteenth-century phrase, "a vast desert."

Today the Great Dismal Swamp National Wildlife Refuge encompasses 107,000 acres in Virginia and North Carolina. It was much larger in Byrd's day, no canals had been cut into the swamp in an attempt to drain it, and its vast store of timber (especially Atlantic white cedar) had not begun to be exploited. Roads now cut into the swamp in several places, and there is a network of canals. The hydrology has changed in much of the area as well, and some of the white cedar and cypress stands Byrd described have given way to maples and gums.

Still, visitors taking some of the nature trails in the refuge can occasionally catch glimpses of a wilderness that seems largely unchanged since the early eighteenth century.

There are diverse plant communities in the refuge, including five different forest types (pine, Atlantic white cedar, maple–black gum, tupelo–bald cypress, and sweet gum–oak-poplar), evergreen shrub communities, marsh, and sphagnum bog. A bewildering array of birds (217 different species) can be found there, along with deer, bear, bobcats and smaller mammals, and many different species of reptiles and amphibians. So much for the place being "a vast desert."

Byrd seems not even to have known of the existence of the large (3,100-acre) lake, Lake Drummond, in the middle of the swamp, even though it had been discovered and named at least a decade before the survey. If he had heard of it, he neglected to mention it in either of his two accounts.

Byrd himself saw only the outer fringes of the Great Dismal. The small group of surveyors who did enter the place spent an entire two weeks drawing the line through it. At times the line could only be advanced a little over a mile a day, owing to the difficulty of the terrain. Byrd and others in his party had leisure to sample the easier living to be had in Edenton. Only two decades from the time of the survey, Edenton would become a prosperous, thriving little port for the colony, but in the spring of 1728 Byrd described it as backwards, provincial, and rough. "I believe," he said, "that this is the only metropolis in the Christian or Mahometan world where there is neither church, chapel, mosque, synagogue, or any other place of public worship of any sect or religion whatsoever. What little devotion there may happen to be is much more private than their vices" (*H* 207). (Interestingly enough, Byrd had relatively little to say about privations in Edenton and the generally sorry state of religion and law in North Carolina in the earlier account, *The Secret History*. Here again, Byrd's realization that *The History* was likely to be read by influential Englishmen no doubt played a part in his dismissal of his southerly neighbors as rude and lawless— the better to show off the virtues of his own colony.)

Life was easy in Edenton, according to Byrd—so easy that no one had to work very hard, and so of course no one did. "Provisions here

are extremely cheap and extremely good, so that people may live plentifully at a trifling expense. Nothing is dear but law, physic, and strong
drink, which are all bad in their kind, and the last they get with so
much difficulty that they are never guilty of the sin of suffering it to
sour upon their hands" (*H* 207).

After the surveying party finished drawing the line through the
Great Dismal, Byrd and the others pushed on westward toward the
Nottoway River. They passed Somerton Chapel, leaving it some two
miles north of the dividing line, and so "there was now no place of
public worship left in the whole province of North Carolina" (*H* 211).
At the Blackwater River Byrd directed the surveyors to drop the line
a half-mile southward, bringing it to the mouth of that river and closer
to the latitude of 36°30′ N agreed upon by John Lawson and other earlier surveyors. From the confluence of the Blackwater and the Nottoway, the line once more continued due west.

By 5 April Byrd had crossed the Meherrin River, very close to the
spot where North Carolina 186 crosses it today. The river itself was
(and still is) narrow and twisting, with low, swampy ground on both
sides, but the higher ground away from the river has deep, sandy soil.
Byrd commented several times on the richness of the plant life and the
productivity of the few farms the group encountered. By this time the
weather had warmed, the men were tired, and the party agreed to put
off finishing their survey until the fall. "Because the spring was now
pretty forward," Byrd explained, "and the rattlesnakes began to crawl
out of their winter quarters and might grow dangerous both to the
men and their horses, it was determined to proceed no farther with the
line till the fall. Besides, the uncommon fatigue the people had under-
gone for near six weeks together and the inclination they all had to
visit their respective families made a recess highly reasonable" (*H* 216).

Among the more interesting specimens of wildlife Byrd mentions
seeing in this section of the survey are wolves and Carolina parakeets.
The parakeets are now extinct, as are the passenger pigeons he describes in later sections. The wolves, which he describes as following
the progress of the line in order to feast on the scraps left behind by
the men as they camped, were until recently entirely extirpated from
both North Carolina and Virginia, and by the 1970s they had been

declared extinct in the wild. (The only breeding populations left were in captivity.) In the 1980s they were reintroduced into the Alligator River National Wildlife Refuge, and there is now a small but slowly growing population in the wild again.

Some of Byrd's most interesting observations in this section are in regard to the Native Americans the group encountered. Here, as in other sections of both *The History* and *The Secret History,* Byrd suggests that the English settlers might have done much better to have taken Indian wives and thereby mingled the bloods of the races, rather than treating the native inhabitants as they had, with suspicion, condescension, and hostility. Not only would wars with Indians have been avoided (the Tuscarora war in North Carolina was a particularly vivid and bloody recent memory), but the number of "his majesty's subjects" in both provinces would have been vastly increased. Even Christianity might have prospered more quickly in the backcountry, "for, after all that can be said, a sprightly lover is the most prevailing missionary that can be sent amongst these or any other infidels" (*H* 160).

While Byrd's comments about the advisability of marriage with the Indians sometimes sound whimsical or half-joking, he had a serious political purpose in mind. He knew that the French had treated the Native Americans much better than their English counterparts had, and at this uncertain time, even on the southern frontier, the French were still very much the feared enemy. Byrd hints in *The History*—and states more plainly in *The Secret History*—that at least some members of his party took Indian lovers during their visit with the Nottoways. There appear to have been no attempts at propagating the gospel or discussing politics during these amours, however.

5 MARCH 1728

The day being now come on which we had agreed to meet the commissioners of North Carolina, we embarked very early, which we could the easier do, having no temptation to stay where we were. We shaped our course along the south end of Knott's Island, there being no passage open on the north. Farther still to the southward of us we discovered two smaller islands that go by the names of Bell's and Church's Isles. We also

saw a small New England sloop riding in the sound a little to
the south of our course. She had come in at the new inlet, as all
other vessels have done since the opening of it. This navigation
is a little difficult and fit only for vessels that draw no more than
ten feet of water. The trade hither is engrossed by the saints of
New England, who carry off a great deal of tobacco without
troubling themselves with paying that impertinent duty of a
penny a pound.

It was just noon before we arrived at Currituck Inlet, which
is now so shallow that the breakers fly over it with a horrible
sound and at the same time afford a very wild prospect. On the
north side of the inlet the high land terminated in a bluff point,
from which a spit of sand extended itself toward the southeast
full half a mile. The inlet lies between that spit and another on
the south side of it, leaving an opening of not quite a mile,
which at this day is not practicable for any vessel whatsoever.
And as shallow as it now is, it continues to fill up more and
more, both the wind and waves rolling in the sands from the
eastern shoals.

About two o'clock in the afternoon we were joined by two of
the Carolina commissioners, attended by Mr. S[wan]n, their surveyor. The other two were not quite so punctual, which was the
more unlucky for us because there could be no sport til they
came. These gentlemen, it seems, had the Carolina commission
in their keeping, notwithstanding which they could not forbear
paying too much regard to a proverb fashionable in their country—not to make more haste than good speed.

However, that we who were punctual might not spend our
precious time unprofitably, we took the several bearings of the
coast. We also surveyed part of the adjacent high land, which
had scarcely any trees growing upon it but cedars. Among the
shrubs, we were showed here and there a bush of Carolina tea
called yaupon, which is one species of phillyrea. This is an evergreen, the leaves whereof have some resemblance to tea but differ widely both in taste and flavor. We also found some few
plants of the spired-leaf silk grass, which is likewise an ever-

green, bearing on a lofty stem a large cluster of flowers of a pale yellow. Of the leaves of this plant the people hereabouts twist very strong cordage.

A virtuoso might divert himself here very well in picking up shells of various hue and figure and amongst the rest that species of conch shell which the Indian peak is made of. The extremities of these shells are blue and the rest white, so that peak of both these colors are drilled out of one and the same shell, serving the natives both for ornament and money, and are esteemed by them far beyond gold and silver (*H* 175–78).

Knott's Island

The island was at this time, as Byrd himself soon discovered, really a large, fertile peninsula, nearly cut off from the mainland by an expanse of low marshland. It is now an island, as a man-made canal separates it from the mainland. Much of the island is low marsh, almost flooded at high tide, and the vast majority of this marshland has become a part of Mackay Island National Wildlife Refuge. The refuge is managed as a wintering ground for thousands of ducks, Canada geese, snow geese, and tundra swans.

The higher ground supports forests of pine, oak, and cedar. Today the island is home to a fishing and farming community. It is linked to the mainland by North Carolina 615, which leads north into the suburbs of Virginia Beach, and by a free ferry at the south end, which connects the island to the little town of Currituck, North Carolina, five miles across the sound.

The whole peninsula is surrounded by the very shallow waters of Back Bay and Currituck Sound. In winter these shallow sounds are particularly attractive to waterfowl, and during the nineteenth and early twentieth centuries both Currituck Sound and Back Bay became famous for their duck and goose hunting. They are still fertile hunting areas, and sportsmen also come to fish for largemouth bass in the sounds. The many duck blinds that dot the water to the horizon testify to the popularity of waterfowl hunting still to be found in the area, but most of the fabulous old hunting clubs, with their huge lodges and caretakers, have disappeared.

I have watched many sunrises from duck blinds in Currituck Sound, sometimes not very far from where the 1728 survey party drew the boundary line. One element making the area so popular with waterfowl is the shallowness of the water—a fact Byrd notes with some displeasure. "We found this navigation very difficult," he says, "by reason of the continued shoals and often stuck fast aground; for though the sound spreads many miles, yet it is in most places extremely shallow and requires a skillful pilot to steer even a canoe over it" (*H* 181). It is, indeed, an unusual experience to sit in a blind built on poles a half mile or more from shore and then to step out of the blind into water only knee deep. These miles of shallows, though, are extremely fertile feeding grounds for ducks, geese, and swans, since they can feed on plants and small marine animals on the bottom without having to dive to great depths.

Currituck Inlet

Just when this inlet appeared and became navigable is anyone's guess. There is no mention of it in early accounts of the area. The 1584 and 1587 expeditions of Sir Walter Raleigh's parties used an inlet to the south, which they called Trinity Inlet. Geographical features along these sandy barrier islands, however, are subject to the whims of storms, and by the middle 1600s Trinity Inlet had disappeared and Currituck Inlet had replaced it as a way into the sounds. John White's late sixteenth-century *Map of Raleigh's Virginia* (extending from just north of the mouth of Chesapeake Bay south to the end of the North Carolina Outer Banks) and his *Chart of all the Coast of Virginia* show several unnamed inlets—most of them now vanished—including one which might be Currituck. It appears about halfway between Trinity Inlet and the mouth of the Chesapeake. A map drawn in 1733 shows Currituck Inlet and also the "new inlet" Byrd mentions, about five miles south of the line. *A New and Accurate Map of North Carolina in North America,* published in *The London Times* in 1843, shows no inlet at the line, but it does show a "New Currituck Inlet" five miles to the south. By 1728, as Byrd notes, Currituck Inlet too was rapidly shoaling in and becoming less navigable, and all shipping was entering the sounds by the "new" inlet that had opened up during a violent storm in 1713.

Today, all the territory immediately to the north of Byrd's line looks very much the way it did in 1728. Byrd would not find any trace of the inlet now, but the low, brushy vegetation clinging to the sand dunes would be familiar looking, as would the forests of oak and cedar further back and the marshes along the sound. The wild horses probably appeared after Byrd's time; at least he makes no mention of them in either of his accounts.

Past the little community of houses clustered within a few hundred yards of the state line at Corova Beach, the area looks unchanged to the south as well. Swimmers and surfers in front of these houses seem oddly isolated, their beach umbrellas sprouting like improbable mushrooms in the sand. A line of tire tracks below the high-tide mark links them to other swimmers, umbrellas, and houses ten miles away, below the wildlife refuge.

A modern visitor to the area can get a good idea of what Byrd saw by hiking into False Cape State Park. With 4,321 acres of land, no vehicular access, and nearly six miles of ocean beach, the park offers at least the illusion of genuine isolation—a rare commodity on oceanfront property anywhere in the Southeast. An interior trail and a number of hiking trails branching off it allow exploration of the maritime forest and the marshes and dunes. (The trail is closed from 1 November until 1 March every year.) Some visitors hike down the ocean beach at low tide, when the walking is easier, and a few reach the area by boat from Back Bay.

Cedars

Byrd refers to both the common red cedar *(Juniperus virginiana)* and the Atlantic white cedar *(Chamaecyparis thyoides)* frequently in his two accounts. The trees are similar in appearance, but the latter (often called "juniper" or just "white cedar") grows in swampy soils like those preferred by the cypress. The cedars Byrd mentions here are red cedars. Much of Currituck National Wildlife Refuge is covered with thickets of low-growing red cedar, with the trees becoming shorter and more shrublike the nearer they grow to the ocean.

Like cypress, both red and white cedar are valued for their resistance to rot, and white cedar especially has long been a prized wood for boatbuilding. In fact, the boatbuilding industry was so dependent on white cedar from coastal Carolina and Virginia that huge stands of it were wiped out. It is now common only in certain wilderness areas, including the Dismal Swamp and the Alligator River National Wildlife Refuge. Byrd frequently comments on the stands of white cedar in his account of the Great Dismal Swamp. See the comments on white cedar and what he calls "juniper" in the entry for 10 March, below.

Yaupon

The yaupon is a very common evergreen shrub in southeastern Virginia and all of coastal North Carolina. It has oblong, leathery leaves and grows to a height of more than fifteen feet. As Byrd notes, it has been used since early colonial times in the making of tea (or at least of a substitute for tea), especially in North Carolina. The earliest reference to the plant comes from Philip Amadas, who in 1584 described Indians on Roanoke Island using yaupon to flavor their water for drinking. The plant bears the unwholesome sounding Latin name *Ilex vomitoria*.

Even in the mid-twentieth century, the more remote islands in the chain called the Outer Banks were relatively isolated from the mainland. There were no bridges connecting Hatteras Island to the mainland, and there was no paved road running the length of either Hatteras or Ocracoke Island. One could choose to bump along on a ribbon of World War II landing mats placed on the sand as a makeshift road or to drive the hard sand on the beach at low tide. As a result of the isolation, some of the habits of earlier centuries persisted in these places, and the use of yaupon tea as a beverage was one of them. When I was a child living on Roanoke Island in the early 1950s, drinking yaupon was associated with hard times and poverty, and I did not know until I was grown that it was supposed to be medicinal. (Calling someone a "yaupon eater" back then was a good way to get a fistfight started.) Just for the record, yaupon has a very strong, acrid taste—not much like tea, at least in my judgment. Byrd seems to concur. He notes in *The Secret History* that yaupon "passes for tea in North Carolina, though nothing like it" (56). Native American medicinal use called for an extremely strong concoction of the stuff, and I have no doubt that it would produce vomiting, as its Latin name implies.

Yaupon is still used occasionally in folk medicine, but rarely as a beverage to replace tea. It is perhaps unique among North American plants in containing caffeine. According to Stephen Foster and James A. Duke, Native Americans in coastal areas used it "as a ceremonial cleansing beverage, drinking large amounts to induce vomiting or act as a purgative" (232).

Spired-leaf silk grass

The plant Byrd describes is a member of the *Yucca* family and grows on sandy beaches and in old fields along the coastal plain from Georgia to southern New Jersey. The leaves, which are generally spear shaped, have long, twisting threads growing from their edges, as the Latin name, *Yucca filamentosa,* suggests. Byrd is correct in his estimation of the use of the plant. Early settlers often used the strong fibers, which can be stripped lengthwise from the leaves, as threads. The threads could be twisted or woven.

Thomas Harriot, in *A Briefe and True Report of the New Found Land of Virginia,* published in 1590, enthusiastically described "silke of grasse or grasse silk" as a wild plant that would lend itself to cultivation for profit. "There is a kind of grasse in the countrey," he wrote, "uppon the blades where of there groweth very good silke in forme of a thin glittering skin to bee stript of. It groweth two foote and a halfe high or better: the blades are about two foot in length, and half inch broad" (7).

Peak

Native Americans used the colorful interiors of certain seashells as trade goods and decorative objects. Clamshells and what Byrd calls "conch shells" (really the shells of whelks) have a particularly attractive, deep blue color along their interior edges, fading to white at the center. Helen Rountree describes the beads of peak as "highly polished and cylindrical, with an average length of one-third inch and diameter of one-quarter inch" (73). She distinguishes between true peak (made of the shells of a clam—*Venus mercenaria*) and other kinds of beads, including those made of conch and mussel shells. Byrd, however, seems to lump the categories together.

According to Byrd, these "conch" shells were drilled and then placed on strings or interwoven with the hair of native women. The three kinds of whelks common in the area are knobbed whelks *(Buccinum carica)*, channeled whelks *(B. canalicatum)*, and lightning whelks *(B. contrarium)*. The first is heavily ridged on its top, and the first and second are "right-handed": that is, the shells open on their right-hand sides. The lightning whelk also has knobs or ridges, but it is a lefty.

6 MARCH 1728

Whilst we were busied about these necessary matters, our skipper rowed to an oyster bank just by and loaded his piragua with oysters as savory and well-tasted as those from Colchester or Walfleet, and had the advantage of them, too, by being much larger and fatter. . . .

While we continued here, we were told that on the south shore not far from the inlet dwelt a marooner that modestly called himself a hermit, though he forfeited that name by suffering a wanton female to cohabit with him. His habitation was a bower covered with bark after the Indian fashion, which in that mild situation protected him pretty well from the weather. Like the ravens, he neither plowed nor sowed but subsisted chiefly upon oysters, which his handmaid made a shift to gather from the adjacent rocks. Sometimes, too, for change of diet, he sent her to drive up the neighbor's cows, to moisten their mouths with a little milk. But as for raiment, he depended mostly upon his length of beard and she upon her length of hair, part of which she brought decently forward and the rest dangled behind quite down to her rump, like one of Herodotus' East Indian Pygmies. Thus did these wretches live in a dirty state of nature and were mere Adamites, innocence only excepted (*H* 178–80).

Oysters

Long a major component of the seafood industry in both North Carolina and Virginia (and long before that an important food item for Indians and colonists), Atlantic oysters *(Crassostrea virginica)* from this area of the coast seem particularly salty and full flavored. In recent years, a severe reduction in the number of these bivalves available locally (a possible result of overharvesting and periodic outbreak of disease) has caused marine biologists at the Virginia Institute of Marine Sciences in Wachapreague to conduct research on ways of finding faster-growing, more disease-resistant strains.

Byrd's description of a hermit or "marooner" and his mistress who live almost exclusively on oysters is no doubt an exaggeration, but it only demonstrates his conviction that life along the line was so easy that one had only to pick up Nature's bounty to be well (if not variously) fed.

7 MARCH 1728

The line cut Dosier's Island, consisting only of a flat sand with here and there an humble shrub growing upon it. From thence it crossed over a narrow arm of the sound into Knott's Island and there split a plantation belonging to William Harding.

The soil is good in many places of this island, and the extent of it pretty large. It lies in the form of a wedge: the south end of it is several miles over, but toward the north it sharpens into a point. It is a plentiful place for stock by reason of the wide marshes adjacent to it and because of its warm situation. But the inhabitants pay a little dear for this convenience by losing as much blood in the summer season by the infinite number of mosquitoes as all their beef and pork can recruit in the winter (*H* 180–81).

"The soil is good"

The higher ground on Knott's Island is very rich and almost black. Nearly every house has a vegetable garden, and the plants grow profusely. As Byrd points out, however, the arable soil is surrounded by swampland and salt marsh, much of it covered with reeds. The mosquitoes coming out of these marshes may not cause quite as much blood loss as he suggests here, but they can still make life uncomfortable when the breeze dies.

8 MARCH 1728

By break of day we sent away our largest piragua with the baggage round the south end of Knott's Island, with orders to the men to wait for us in the mouth of North River. Soon after, we embarked ourselves on board the smaller vessel, with intent, if possible, to find a passage round the north end of the island. . . .

It was discovered by this day's work that Knott's Island was improperly so called, being in truth no more than a peninsula. The northwest side of it is only divided from the main by the great marsh above-mentioned, which is seldom overflowed. Instead of that, it might by the labor of a few trenches be drained into firm meadow, capable of grazing as many cattle as Job in his best estate was master of. In the miry condition it now lies, it feeds great numbers in the winter, though when the weather grows warm they are driven from thence by the mighty armies of mosquitoes, which are the plague of the lower part of Carolina as much as flies were formerly of Egypt (and some rabbis think those flies were no other than mosquitoes) (*H* 181–82).

"It might by the labor of a few trenches be drained"

Byrd had little use for "pocosins," or swamps. He saw them as impediments to progress and detrimental to commerce and agriculture. Today, most people with any interest in the outdoors realize that marshes and wetlands, especially estuarine marshes such as the ones surrounding Knott's Island, are not only rich with life but also extremely important breeding and feeding grounds for a host of marine animals. While marshes and other valuable wetlands continue to disappear all over the Southeast, some progress has been made in the last quarter of a century at slowing the rate of loss.

Much of Knott's Island now is a part of the Mackay Island National Wildlife Refuge, and the refuge status affords protection to this valuable natural resource. The refuge includes 8,646 acres of land in North Carolina and Virginia, and the vast majority of it (over 6,000 acres) is made up of wetlands. Up to seventy-five thousand visitors come every year, many of them to look at the great variety of waterbirds and songbirds that use the refuge. In 1728, the only species of wildlife Byrd even mentioned in this vast wetland was the mosquito.

9 MARCH 1728

The surveyors entered early upon their business this morning and ran the line through Mr. Eyland's plantation, as far as the banks of North River. They passed over it in the piragua and landed in Gibb's marsh, which was a mile in breadth and tolerably firm. They trudged through this marsh without difficulty as far as the high land, which promised more fertility than any they had seen in these lower parts. But this firm land lasted not long before they came upon the dreadful pocosin they had been threatened with. Nor did they find it one jot better than it had been painted to them. The beavers and otters had rendered it quite impassable for any creatures but themselves (*H* 182–83).

Pocosin

"Pocosin" is a Native American term for "swamp." Literature distributed by the U.S. Fish and Wildlife Service translates the word as "swamp on a hill," and the term is usually used today to refer to a swamp in an upland coastal region. Typically, pocosins are places with tangled, low-growing vegetation and a scattered overstory of pond pine. Walking in such areas is extremely difficult; walking in a straight line, such as one would have to do if one were making a survey, is a great deal harder still. There is now a large (111,000-acre) refuge just south of Albemarle Sound called Pocosin Lakes National Wildlife Refuge. Byrd uses the term indiscriminately to refer to any particularly difficult swamp.

Beavers and otters

Both animals were very common in the swamps during Byrd's lifetime, and they are common once again today. Beavers *(Castor canadensis)* declined during the late eighteenth and nineteenth centuries as a result of excessive trapping for the fur trade, and by the early twentieth century they had been almost exterminated in both North Carolina and Virginia. Thanks to massive livetrapping and relocation efforts begun in the 1930s, their numbers have rebounded. In some sections of both states, beavers are now numerous enough to present minor problems. They flood low-lying tracts of commercial timber, invade private ponds, and destroy decorative plantings of dogwood and other trees in the front yards of lakeside vacation homes. Byrd was absolutely correct in his judgment that beaver swamps made for excruciatingly difficult walking.

River otters *(Lutra canadensis),* which may inhabit the same swamps as beavers, are fish eaters and do not drop trees or drag large limbs into the water, thereby impeding foot traffic for surveyors and other non-swamp dwellers. Like beavers, otters have made a dramatic comeback in recent years. Both beavers and otters can now be found in most counties along the line as well as within the city limits of several major metropolitan areas in both North Carolina and Virginia.

10 MARCH 1728

We observed very few cornfields in our walks and those very small, which seemed the stranger to us because we could see no other tokens of husbandry or improvement. But upon further inquiry we were given to understand people only made corn for themselves and not for their stocks, which know very well how to get their own living. Both cattle and hogs ramble into the neighboring marshes and swamps, where they maintain themselves the whole winter long and are not fetched home till the spring. Thus do these indolent wretches during one half of the year lose the advantage of the milk of their cattle, as well as their dung, and many of the poor creatures perish in the mire, into the bargain, by this ill management. Some who pique themselves more upon industry than their neighbors will now and then, in compliment to their cattle, cut down a tree whose limbs are loaded with the moss aforementioned. The trouble would be too great to climb the tree in order to gather this provender, but the shortest way (which in this country is always counted the best) is to fell it, just like the lazy Indians, who do the same by such trees as bear fruit and so make one harvest for all (*H* 184).

Cattle and hogs

The habit of letting stock roam freely persisted in parts of the Southeast well into the twentieth century. An inevitable result was that some animals escaped, reproduced, and established a population of feral cattle and hogs. Wild hogs are still relatively common along the northernmost Outer Banks of North Carolina and in the False Cape area of Virginia. They are, in fact, common enough to be regarded as a serious nuisance, since they destroy erosion-preventing vegetation by their rooting and compete for food with native species such as deer and squirrels. Both False Cape State Park and Back Bay National Wildlife Refuge have opened limited seasons with carefully controlled hunts in an attempt to limit the damage done by hogs to native vegetation. Currituck National Wildlife Refuge has authorized no such controlled hunting yet, but this area is surrounded by large tracts of privately owned land, where some hunting does take place. Still, a conversation with the manager of Currituck in the summer of 1999 revealed that damage by hogs in the refuge is a growing problem.

Hogs are remarkably adaptable animals, and they are able to eat a wide variety of plants and whatever animals they can unearth, catch, or subdue. Farmers with more labor-intensive crops to attend to (including tobacco and cotton) would often allow their hogs to roam in the woods and swamps, rounding them up when they were needed. A common method of getting the animals back was by baiting them into catch pens with corn.

Both cattle and hogs, but especially hogs, were often marked by notching the ears in a distinctive fashion, so that a farmer could determine that a free-range sow with notched ears and a litter of piglets belonged to him and not to his neighbor. My father-in-law, Loyd Claburn, grew up during the depression era in southern Mississippi, where open-range practices were still common. His family's mark was a "double fork right and a swallow tail left"—ear-notch patterns that clearly identified the semiferal stock. Stock was sometimes rounded up by using dogs, including a "catch-dog," which was often a large bull-dog or bulldog mix that would grab the snout of a hog or the muzzle of a cow and not let go until handlers could come to its aid.

In many areas of the South today, descendants of such free-range hogs have multiplied and become a mixed blessing for wildlife-management departments. On the one hand, the hogs compete directly with native animals, including deer, bears, and squirrels. They also destroy many plants with their rooting, and their habit of eating whatever amphibians and reptiles they can catch in the process sometimes threatens rare species. On the other hand, many sportsmen are enthusiastic about hunting for the animals, and consequently the hogs bring in much-needed revenues to game departments interested in managing a wide range of species.

Having hunted wild hogs in several places, I can attest to their ability to fend very well for themselves in almost any environment. They tend to be leaner than domestic hogs, with highly developed survival instincts, and they can run nearly as fast as deer over short distances. (A boar running directly at you, by the way, seems to move alarmingly fast. I have two vivid memories of such head-on views.) Adult wild hogs in the southeastern United States have no natural enemies except alligators. Bobcats and occasionally bears may feed on young pigs.

Wild cattle have been largely exterminated from the area, but feral horses are common, especially in the Currituck National Wildlife Refuge, and are regarded as either vegetation-destroying menaces or valuable tourist attractions, depending on one's point of view. There were until fairly recently a few wild cattle on the islands of the lower Outer Banks, but the National Park Service has succeeded in removing them.

"Whose limbs are loaded with the moss aforementioned"

Byrd encountered trees with "long moss dangling from their branches" in the low country of Virginia before he reached the line and more frequently the further south he went. Such moss is still plentiful in some lowland areas between the boundary line and Edenton, North Carolina, the southernmost point of Byrd's 1728 visit. He was convinced that "both cattle and horses eat this moss greedily in winter when other provender is scarce, though it is apt to scour them at first" (H 172).

Spanish moss *(Tillandsia usneoides)* is a tropical plant that grows in profusion on both sides of the survey line in extreme southeastern Vir-

ginia and northeastern North Carolina. According to A. M. Harvill, Jr.,
it can be found in the southeastern border counties of Virginia but is
much more prominent along the Carolina line and southward. One of
the best places near the line to see great masses of the stuff now is at
Merchant's Millpond State Park, just south of the Virginia line along
U.S. 158, in Gates County.

Byrd's note that cattle and horses eat the moss "greedily in winter" may be an exaggeration. Spanish moss has very little food value.
While farmers have occasionally used it as a substitute for hay, it is not
so nourishing that a well-fed animal would prefer it to almost any
other food. Spanish moss does have limited commercial use today, but
not as animal food. It is gathered, bound in bales, and used for stuffing
furniture. The moss is also used in floral decorations.

11 MARCH 1728

We ordered the surveyors early to their business, who were
blessed with pretty dry grounds for three miles together. But
they paid dear for it in the next two, consisting of one continued
frightful pocosin, which no creatures but those of the amphibious kind ever had ventured into before. This filthy quagmire did
in earnest put the men's courage to a trial, and though I can't say
it made them lose their patience, yet they lost their humor for
joking. They kept their gravity like so many Spaniards, so that a
man might have taken his opportunity to plunge up to the chin
without danger of being laughed at. However, this unusual composure of countenance could not fairly be called complaining.

Their day's work ended at the mouth of Northern's Creek,
which empties itself into Northwest River; though we chose to
quarter a little higher up the river near Mossy Point. This we did
for the convenience of an old house to shelter our persons and
baggage from rain, which threatened us hard.

We had encamped so early that we found time in the evening
to walk near half a mile into the woods. There we came upon a
family of mulattoes that called themselves free, though by the
shyness of the master of the house, who took care to keep least
in sight, their freedom seemed a little doubtful. It is certain many

slaves shelter themselves in this obscure part of the world, nor will any of their righteous neighbors discover them. On the contrary, they find their account in settling such fugitives on some out-of-the-way corner of their land to raise stocks for a mean and inconsiderable share, well knowing their condition makes it necessary for them to submit to any terms (*H* 185–86).

Northwest River

This small blackwater stream, lined with cypress trees in its upper reaches and flowing through marshes a few miles before emptying into Currituck Sound, is a popular location for freshwater fishing today. Byrd's reference to "Moss Point" is doubtless an indication of the Spanish moss that grows on much of the cypress and pine along parts of the river. Northwest River Park, just off Virginia 168 in extreme southern Chesapeake County, Virginia, provides camping, boating, hiking trails, and an elevated walkway over the marsh and cypress swamp. A small, scenic campground, located about a half mile north of the line, almost at the spot where the party camped, offers easy access to the river.

Slaves

At various locations throughout the wilder parts of the South, especially in isolated, swampy areas, there were families or even small communities of escaped slaves. The vast wilderness area south of the Albemarle Sound was one such location, southeastern North Carolina's Green Swamp was another, and, as Byrd points out, the edge of the Dismal Swamp along the Carolina-Virginia line was a third. Bland Simpson devotes over eight pages of his *The Great Dismal: A Swamp Memoir* to stories of runaway slaves in the Dismal Swamp. Simpson speculates that Byrd may have seen the beginnings of a long-lasting community of runaways and their descendants during the 1728 survey (69–77).

The Dismal was a well-known haven for escaped slaves until the end of the Civil War, over a century and a quarter later. Simpson cites an account of a black outlaw named Tom Copper in 1802, who "stirred fears of a Negro insurrection" (115).

13 MARCH 1728

Early this morning our chaplain repaired to us with the men we had left at Mr. Wilson's. We had sent for them the evening before to relieve those who had the labor oar from Currituck Inlet. But to our great surprise, they petitioned not to be relieved, hoping to gain immortal reputation by being the first of mankind that ventured through the Great Dismal. But the rest being equally ambitious of the same honor, it was but fair to decide their portions by lot. . . .

In the meanwhile, the surveyors carried the line three miles, which was no contemptible day's work, considering how cruelly they were entangled with briers and gallbushes. The leaf of this last shrub bespeaks it to be of the alaternus family.

Our work ended within a quarter of a mile of the Dismal aforementioned, where the ground began to be already full of sunken holes and slashes, which had, here and there, some few reeds growing in them. 'Tis hardly credible how little the bordering inhabitants were acquainted with this mighty swamp, notwithstanding they had lived their whole lives within smell of it. Yet, as great strangers as they were to it, they pretended to be very exact in their account of its dimensions and were positive it could not be above seven or eight miles wide, but knew no more of the matter than stargazers know of the distance of the fixed stars. At the same time, they were simple enough to amuse our men with idle stories of the lions, panthers, and alligators they were likely to encounter in that dreadful place. In short, we saw plainly there was no intelligence of this Terra Incognita to be got but from our own experience (*H* 187–88).

Gallbushes

There are two closely related species of gallberry ("gallbushes") growing in the area, and Byrd possibly lumped the two together, as they are very similar in appearance. Both the bitter gallberry (*Ilex glabra,* also called inkberry) and the sweet or giant gallberry *(I. coriacea)* form a thick understory in the low, swampy soil of southeastern Virginia and northeastern North Carolina (Fernald 982). The inkberry is more

widely distributed, however, growing in coastal areas occasionally as
far north as Maine; it is very common in the coastal plain of Virginia.
Giant gallberry grows from about the Virginia line southward, and,
while its leaves, bark, and foliage look very much like those of the
inkberry, it reaches heights of twenty feet or more. Byrd mentions the
plant (or plants) several times, not always as an obstacle to progress. In
The History he describes it as "a beautiful evergreen" that "may be cut
into any shape," adding that when it is transplanted into gardens, "it
will not thrive without frequent watering" (172). This is another indication that he may be confusing the two gallberries; the inkberry has
often been used as an ornamental shrub, but the larger, more open-
crowned giant gallberry would be relatively unsuited for cutting "into
any shape." In *The Secret History* he describes the bushes as "evergreen
shrubs bearing a berry which dyes a black color like the galls of oak,
and from thence they receive their name" (*SH* 70).

Lions, panthers, and alligators

Byrd's tendency to doubt stories about panthers (actually cougars;
real panthers are a different genus, *Panthera*) and alligators comes only
from his belief that no animal of any kind lived in the Great Dismal
Swamp. As we can see from later entries in both *The History* and *The
Secret History,* he regards panthers as fairly ordinary, and he discusses
both panthers and alligators with enthusiasm, relating a mixture of
fact and fantasy about the latter. The eastern cougar *(Felis concolor),* also
known as the mountain lion or puma, has been listed as endangered
east of the Mississippi River since the early twentieth century, and it is
extinct over the vast majority of its former range. The Florida panther,
which is another, slightly smaller subspecies *(Felis concolor coryi)* holds
on with a population of perhaps a hundred or more animals, most of
them in extreme southern Florida.

Reports of panther sightings from the southern Appalachians
and from large expanses of coastal wilderness in the Carolinas and Virginia persist and have actually increased in recent years, but no solid,
incontrovertible evidence of the great cat's existence there has yet
emerged. The U.S. Fish and Wildlife Service recorded sightings in the
Smoky Mountains National Park in the mid-1970s, and a very few in

other locations in North Carolina, Virginia, and West Virginia since that time. Cougars certainly inhabited the Dismal Swamp during the eighteenth century, however. (For a discussion of the possible presence or absence of cougars in Virginia and North Carolina at the present time, see the more lengthy comments on the animals for the entry of 18 October, below.)

Byrd's reference to lions is probably intended as a joke at the expense of the storytellers' credulity, but in fact the word *lion* was sometimes used by early explorers and settlers to describe the panther. Thomas Harriot described the diets and hunting of the Roanoke Island natives, who "sometimes hunt the lyon, and eat him" (20).

All of Byrd's comments on the inhospitable nature of the Great Dismal Swamp can be summed up in a single sentence from *The Secret History:* "It is remarkable that toward the middle of the Dismal no beast or bird or even reptile can live, not only because of the softness of the ground but likewise because 'tis so overgrown with thickets that the genial beams of the sun can never penetrate them" (*SH* 70).

Alligators

Again, Byrd was basing his doubts on the conviction that not even reptiles lived in the Great Dismal. He also thought birds avoided flying over it. Alligators *(Alligator mississippiensis)* are found at the present time approximately fifty miles south of Byrd's line, in the Alligator River National Wildlife Refuge. This probably represents the extreme northern range of the species, at least of breeding populations, though isolated animals occasionally turn up north of the Albemarle Sound and almost to southern Virginia (Palmer and Braswell 271; O'Brien and Doerr 447). Martof et al. speculate that in previous centuries alligators may have inhabited the Great Dismal Swamp, but they do not say what evidence this speculation is based on (144). Byrd's contemporary John Lawson once built a house on top of an alligator hole and was awakened by the animal's bellowing one March night in 1701. This happened near the Neuse River, in Craven County, North Carolina, about one hundred miles south of the line, where the animals were much more common (Savage 40). See also the comments after Byrd's description of Carolina alligators on 15 November, below.

14 MARCH 1728

Although there was no need of example to inflame persons already so cheerful, yet to enter the people with the better grace, the author and two more of the commissioners accompanied them half a mile into the Dismal. The skirts of it were thinly planted with dwarf reeds and gallbushes, but when we got into the Dismal itself we found the reeds grew much taller and closer and, to mend the matter, were so interlaced with bamboo briers that there was no scuffling through them without the help of pioneers. At the same time, we found the ground moist and trembling under our feet like a quagmire, insomuch that it was an easy matter to run a ten-foot pole up to the head in it without exerting any uncommon strength to do it. . . .

At the same time they were laboring with their hands to cut down the reeds, which were ten feet high, their legs were hampered with briers. Besides, the weather happened to be warm, and the tallness of the reeds kept off every friendly breeze from coming to refresh them. And indeed it was a little provoking to hear the wind whistling among the branches of the white cedars, which grew here and there amongst the reeds, and at the same time not to have the comfort to feel the least breath of it (*H* 189–90).

Reeds

Byrd's surveyors often found themselves in dense thickets of reeds that stretched for miles. Such reed thickets are still very common in certain sections of the Great Dismal Swamp, especially south of Lake Drummond. The plant described here is the common reed, *Phragmites communis*, which reaches a height of twelve feet or more in the swampy soil. Seeing over or through the reeds when one is in the middle of the kind of thicket Byrd describes is usually impossible, and it is easy to become disoriented.

Though Byrd himself did not go far enough into the swamp to see the reeds at their highest and thickest (having spent some time in the town of Edenton while the survey team hacked its way through the swamp), his reports indicate that the men could sometimes see noth-

ing around them but a vast sea of reeds. In *The Secret History* he refers
to a section of the Dismal as the "Green Sea": "Some part of this swamp
has few or no trees growing in it but contains a large tract of reeds,
which being perpetually green and waving in the wind, it is called the
Green Sea" (*SH* 70).

15 MARCH 1728

The surveyors pursued their work with all diligence but still
found the soil of the Dismal so spongy that the water oozed up
into every footstep they took. To their sorrow, too, they found
the reeds and briers more firmly interwoven than they did the
day before. But the greatest grievance was from large cypresses
which the wind had blown down and heaped upon one another.
On the limbs of most of them grew sharp snags, pointing every
way like so many pikes, that required much pains and caution to
avoid. These trees, being evergreens and shooting their large
tops very high, are easily overset by every gust of wind, because
there is no firm earth to steady their roots.

There is but little wool in that province, though cotton grows
very kindly and, so far south, is seldom nipped by the frost. The
good women mix this with their wool for their outer garments;
though, for want of fulling, that kind of manufacture is open and
sleazy. Flax likewise thrives there extremely, being perhaps as
fine as any in the world, and I question not might with a little
care and pains be brought to rival that of Egypt; and yet the
men are here so intolerably lazy they seldom take the trouble
to propagate it (*H* 191–92).

Cypresses

The bald cypress *(Taxodium distichum)* is common all along the
eastern part of Byrd's line, and huge stands of it are to be found in
the Great Dismal Swamp. In very wet soil, or where the lower trunks
of the trees are frequently flooded, the bases of the trees grow much
thicker, fuller, and more porous. Often they send up unbranched
shoots—the familiar "cypress knees." Cypress trees are probably no
more prone to being blown over in high winds than any other trees,

but they are unusual in that a forest fire is likely to burn the lighter bases of the trees, toppling them. The rot-resistant trunks may then last for decades, and Byrd might be excused for thinking that many of the great trees had fallen all at once in a recent storm.

The "spongy soil" Byrd frequently mentions is made up of layers of sphagnum moss (the decayed form is peat moss), which will occasionally smolder and burn during a forest fire, giving the impression that the ground itself is burning. A fire of this sort in a stand of cypress would drop many trees and result in exactly the kind of tangled maze Byrd describes.

Byrd was not correct in calling the cypress an "evergreen." It is deciduous, dropping its needles during the winter and giving rise to its common name, "bald cypress."

Flax

Flax has not been a commercial crop since colonial times, when it was used in the manufacture of clothing. The same flax Byrd describes *(Linum usitatissimum)* occasionally turns up as a weed with light blue flowers, growing "along railroads and roadsides" in eastern Virginia and North Carolina (Radford et al., *Manual,* 645).

Cotton

Cotton *(Gossypium herbaceum)* was a fairly important commercial crop in the eastern part of both North Carolina and Virginia until the early twentieth century, when boll-weevil infestations virtually destroyed the industry almost overnight. Farmers turned quickly to more profitable, safer crops, including tobacco (which had always been of paramount importance in the region anyway), beef cattle, corn, soybeans, and timber production. In the late twentieth century cotton made a remarkable comeback, however, and low country farms on both sides of the border produce vast fields of it.

17 MARCH 1728

Since the surveyors had entered the Dismal, they had laid eyes on no living creature: neither bird nor beast, insect nor reptile came in view. Doubtless the eternal shade that broods over this mighty bog and hinders the sunbeams from blessing the ground makes it an uncomfortable habitation for anything that has life. Not so much as a Zeeland frog could endure so aguish a situation. It had one beauty, however, that delighted the eye, though at the expense of all the other senses: the moisture of the soil preserves a continual verdure and makes every plant an evergreen; but at the same time the foul damps ascend without ceasing, corrupt the air, and render it unfit for respiration. Not even a turkey buzzard will venture to fly over it, no more than the Italian vultures will over the filthy Lake Avernus, or the birds in the Holy Land over the Salt Sea where Sodom and Gomorrah formerly stood (*H* 194).

"Neither bird nor beast, insect nor reptile, came in view"

There are two possible explanations for this and other assertions that the Great Dismal was devoid of life. One is that the surveyors made so much noise and were so thickly surrounded by vegetation that they frightened off whatever wildlife might have been close by and were unable to see any great distance ahead of themselves. Another, more plausible reason may be that Byrd was simply wrong. Even in the dead of winter, it would be almost impossible to spend any time in the Dismal and see neither "bird nor beast, insect nor reptile," and this survey was conducted in the spring. Byrd complains bitterly of "that Carolina scourge, mosquitoes" as well as biting flies at many points along the journey, but he suggests that the center of the great swamp was even free of these life-forms. Anyone who has spent a warm afternoon there must doubt it seriously.

It seems likely, then, that Byrd formed an opinion about the place, based partly on local stories and partly on his preconceived ideas about "noxious vapors" and "poisonous damps," and constructed this portion of the history without questioning his surveyors very closely. Scrupulously honest in most of his own observations of nature, Byrd was apt to rely on hearsay and unsubstantiated tales when describing events or animals (crocodiles, for instance) he had never seen. It is apparently true, however, that the surveyors found no game for food in the swamp during their journey through it. Byrd says in *The Secret*

History that he "had indeed given them a warrant to kill anything that came in their way in case of necessity, not knowing that no living creature could inhabit that inhospitable place" (*SH* 68).

I have visited the great swamp on several occasions, usually going in by boat and exploring the area around Lake Drummond. I never failed to see an abundance of life there, from snakes, turtles, and frogs to birds and mammals. (I found a plentiful supply of insect life, too.) It is, of course, much easier to get into the swamp now than it was in Byrd's day, and incalculably easier to find your way back out once you get in. At various places there are walking trails and even elevated wooden walkways above the swamp, and the canal leading to Lake Drummond is string-straight and plainly marked. Still, at over one hundred thousand acres, the Dismal covers a lot of territory, and there are places in the refuge where one can see the swamp much as Byrd's survey party saw it. It is easy to imagine the difficulty a party would have had in maintaining a straight survey line through such a tangled wilderness without canals, roads, and walkways.

The hydrology of the swamp has also changed radically since Byrd's survey. The first efforts at draining and logging parts of the area began when George Washington organized the Dismal Swamp Land Company sometime after his first visit there in 1763. The entire area has been cut over at least once since then, and logging in some parts of it continued as late as 1976. (Part of the area was first established as a National Wildlife Refuge in 1973.) The roads and canals built to sustain the logging effort have dried out some areas of the swamp, changing the look of the landscape and encouraging different kinds of plant growth. More of it, for instance, is in pine and maple–black gum forests now than would have been the case in the eighteenth century, when vast stands of Atlantic white cedar and tupelo-cypress predominated over much of the area.

I have also spent some time covering similar terrain on private property not far south of the wildlife refuge. My own explorations were usually confined to areas very near navigable streams, since the vegetation was so thick and formidable that I worried I might easily get lost if I ventured more than a few dozen yards into the swamp. Even carrying a compass is no guarantee against finding oneself on the wrong side of an almost impassable bog or a thicket so tightly ingrown that one must cut a way through it. A companion of mine did, in fact, get lost for a little while in exactly the kind of reed thicket that Byrd describes above. He had been following a bear's trail through the reeds and got confused as to which direction and which of several trails he should take to return to the river. After some very loud shouting he managed to alert the rest of us to his general location, and my shouts guided him back to the safety of the river. It made for an amusing story later, but I think I always enjoyed the telling of it more than he did.

19 MARCH 1728
> We ordered several men to patrol on the edge of the Dismal, both toward the north and toward the south, and to fire guns at proper distances. This they performed very punctually but could hear nothing in return nor gain any sort of intelligence. In the meantime, whole flocks of women and children flew thither to stare at us with as much curiosity as if we had lately landed from Bantam or Morocco.
>
> None of our visitors could, however, tell us any news of the surveyors, nor indeed was it possible any of them should at that time, they being still laboring in the midst of the Dismal. It seems they were able to carry the line this day no farther than one mile and sixty-one poles, and that whole distance was through a cedar bog, where the ground trembled under their feet most mightily (*H* 196).

Cedar bog
The cedars referred to here are the swamp-loving Atlantic white cedar, as Byrd makes plain in an entry in *The Secret History* for 23 March: "In other places it was full of juniper trees, commonly so called though they seem to be white cedars. Some of these are of a great bigness, but, the soil being soft and boggy, there is little hold for the roots, and consequently any high wind blows many of them down" (*SH* 67–70).

Atlantic white cedar, which is still locally called juniper, has long been valued for the ease with which it can be worked and for its resistance to rot. In previous centuries posts, roofing shingles, and boats

were often constructed of white cedar, and the demand for it was so
great that most of the supply has now vanished. When I was a child
living on the coast about sixty miles south of the line, skiffs made
of "juniper" were in great demand among local fisherman. My family
owned one such skiff—a heavy but very stable vessel powered by a
small outboard. According to local lore, juniper was even better than
cypress at withstanding the effects of hard use in salt water.

John E. Kuser and George Zimmerman point out that white cedar
is dependent on periodic fires to suppress rival plant communities;
once rivals such as red maples get established, the cedars do not regenerate well. Early silvaculture practices along the Atlantic seaboard sup-
pressed fire, and the great white cedar–swamp forests did not grow
back after being cut. See the discussion of the longleaf pine, another
fire-dependent species, in the comments for 25 March, below.

About 90 percent of the original white cedar–swamp forest area
in North Carolina, and about 98 percent of it in Virginia, has vanished.
The greatest concentration of white cedar now is within the Alligator
River National Wildlife Refuge and in the Great Dismal Swamp Refuge. Efforts are now being made to regenerate white-cedar forests in
several parts of the Southeast.

23 MARCH 1728

By the description the surveyors gave of the Dismal, we were
convinced that nothing but the exceeding dry season we had
been blessed with could have made the passing of it practicable.
It is the source of no less than five several rivers which discharge
themselves southward into Albemarle Sound and of two that run
northerly into Virginia. From thence 'tis easy to imagine that the
soil must be thoroughly soaked with water or else there must be
plentiful stores of it underground to supply so many rivers, especially since there is no lake or any considerable body of that element to be seen on the surface. The rivers that head in it from
Virginia are the south branch of Nansemond and the west branch
of Elizabeth, and those from Carolina Northwest River, North
River, Pasquotank, Little River, and Perquimans (H 202–3).

"There is no lake or any considerable body of that element to be seen on the surface"

That William Byrd was completely ignorant of the existence of a great lake in the middle of the swamp is simply an indication of how wild and relatively unexplored the region was in the early eighteenth century. According to local (and perhaps apocryphal) legend, Governor William Drummond himself first discovered the lake after getting lost on a hunting trip in the Dismal in 1665, nearly seventy years before Byrd's survey. By the nineteenth century the lake had become the subject of romantic etchings (such as those of David Hunter Strother). The Irish poet Thomas Moore wrote his "The Lake of the Dismal Swamp" in 1801.

Lake Drummond is on ground higher than most of the surrounding swamp, and its waters used to sheet all over the swamp in a maze of different directions. As I have noted, the construction of logging roads and canals changed the hydrology of the whole area, but it is still easy to see the difference in elevation of the lake and the surrounding swamp. If you approach the lake from the feeder ditch that leads off the canal running alongside U.S. 17, you must either have your boat locked into the lake or must leave it behind in the canal and walk up a fairly steep little hill.

There are several theories as to how the lake was formed. Probably the most likely is that much of the higher ground in the swamp once dried out in a time of prolonged drought. A forest fire ignited the dried peat that made up the forest floor and, burning for an extended period of time, formed a great depression that filled with water when the rains eventually returned.

Byrd's opinions of the swamp (other than that it was a thoroughly nasty place) were utilitarian. He proposed draining it, cutting canals through it, and logging it—all projects that were partially accomplished a few decades after his survey. "It would require a great sum of money to drain it," he noted, "but the public treasure could not be better bestowed than to preserve the lives of His Majesty's liege people and at the same time render so great a tract of swamp very profitable, besides the advantage of making a channel to transport by water car-

riage goods from Albemarle Sound into Nansemond and Elizabeth
Rivers in Virginia" (*H* 202).

George Washington became interested in the possibility of farming the Dismal, and under his direction some of the draining and canal
construction began. That eighteenth-century American, by the way,
explored the swamp, camped in it, and described it enthusiastically as
"a glorious paradise" just thirty-five years after Byrd's survey (Simpson 41). His efforts to drain and cultivate a large section of it, however,
came to nothing. Today, traffic speeds along U.S. 17 as it parallels the
Dismal Swamp Canal, a branch of the Atlantic Intracoastal Waterway
providing an inland route from the Chesapeake Bay to the Pasquotank
River in North Carolina and from there into Albemarle Sound. A feeder
ditch off the Dismal Swamp Canal leads to Lake Drummond. The lake
is also accessible from its western side via the Washington Ditch Road.

25 MARCH 1728

The soil of our landlord's plantation, though none of the best,
seemed more fertile than any thereabouts, where the ground is
near as sandy as the deserts of Africa and consequently barren.
The road leading from thence to Edenton, being in distance
about twenty-seven miles, lies upon a ridge called Sandy Ridge,
which is so wretchedly poor that it will not grow potatoes. The
pines in this part of the country are of a different species from
those in Virginia: their bearded leaves are much longer and their
cones much larger. Each cell contains a seed of the size and
figure of a black-eyed pea, which, shedding in November, is
very good mast for hogs and fattens them in a short time. The
smallest of these pines are full of cones which are eight or nine
inches long, and each affords commonly sixty or seventy seeds.
This kind of mast has the advantage of all other by being more
constant and less liable to be nipped by the frost or eaten by the
caterpillars.

The trees also abound more with turpentine and consequently
yield more tar than either the yellow or the white pine and for
the same reason make them more durable timber for building.
The inhabitants hereabouts pick up knots of lightwood in abun-

dance, which they burn into tar and then carry it to Norfolk or Nansemond for a market (*H* 203–4).

Pines

Byrd, of course, here describes the stately longleaf pine *(Pinus palustris)*, once a very common tree in the sandy lowlands of North Carolina's coastal plain. It was not found much farther north than the northeastern counties of Carolina. Albert E. Radford et al. record the northernmost trees in Dare and Edgecombe Counties, near the thirty-sixth parallel (*Atlas,* 7). This is about ten miles south of Byrd's location on 25 March, the time of this description. The trees are easily recognizable by their extremely long needles (up to nearly a foot in length) and their large cones, which look somewhat like miniature footballs.

There are few large stands of longleaf pine left in the state now, or anywhere else in the Southeast for that matter. Loblolly pines grow much faster and are generally preferred for timber production, and so the native longleafs have been largely displaced. In fact virtual monocultures of loblolly pine plantations now cover many forested areas in the Southeast. Such monocultures are, by comparison with mixed forests, relatively unsuitable for a diversity of wildlife.

Longleaf pines do best in areas that are subject to periodic fires, whether caused by lightning or set by man. The fires destroy the understory, allowing the young pines (which look like tufts of coarse grass) to compete more successfully. In recent years fire has become a management tool in all kinds of pine plantations, but the naturally occurring wildfires in previous centuries enabled large colonies of longleaf pines to become established. Jeff Beane estimates that by the mid-1950s, nearly 95 percent of the longleaf pines in North Carolina had disappeared (29).

Byrd's comments here and elsewhere about the manufacture of tar from pine trees reflect the growing importance of that industry to North Carolina, which would later be called "the tar heel state."

26 March 1728

Most of the rum they get in this country comes from New England and is so bad and unwholesome that it is not improperly called "kill-devil." It is distilled there from foreign molasses, which, if skillfully managed, yields near gallon for gallon. Their molasses comes from the same country and has the name "long sugar" in Carolina, I suppose from the ropiness of it, and serves all the purposes of sugar, both in their eating and drinking. When they entertain their friends bountifully, they fail not to set before them a capacious bowl of bombo, so called from the admiral of that name. This is a compound of rum and water in equal parts, made palatable with the said long sugar. As good humor begins to flow and the bowl to ebb they take care to re-plenish it with sheer rum, of which there always is a reserve under the table.

Very few in this country have the industry to plant orchards, which in a dearth of rum, might supply them with much better liquor. The truth is, there is one inconvenience that easily dis-courages lazy people from making this improvement: very often, in autumn, when the apples begin to ripen, they are visited with numerous flights of parakeets, that bite all the fruit to pieces in a moment for the sake of the kernels. The havoc they make is sometimes so great that whole orchards are laid waste, in spite of all the noises that can be made to fright 'em away. These rav-enous birds visit North Carolina only during the warm season and so soon as the cold begins to come on retire back toward the sun. They rarely venture so far north as Virginia, except in a very hot summer, when they visit the most southern parts of it. They are very beautiful but, like some other pretty creatures, are apt to be loud and mischievous (*H* 205–6).

Kill-devil

Byrd's off-hand comment on the quality of the whiskey to be had in the province casts light on the origin of the name of a popular re-sort community, Kill Devil Hills, in Dare County, North Carolina.

Parakeets

Byrd describes the Carolina parakeet *(Conuropsis carolinensis),* a magnificently colorful bird that is now extinct. Once so common in the Southeast as to be regarded as a serious pest, the species had nearly vanished by the middle of the nineteenth century. Parakeets came into the Carolinas and occasionally into extreme southern Virginia every summer, and they must have made quite a spectacle of color. A portrait by John James Audubon, painted around 1830, shows seven of the birds feeding on fruit. They are predominantly green, with yellow heads and with touches of russet on the tops of the heads and blue on the outer surfaces of the wings. This was the only parrot species commonly occurring anywhere in North America. It is likely that the parakeets' habit of feeding voraciously on orchards planted by white settlers, thereby concentrating themselves in enormous numbers where they could be more easily killed, helped account for their extirpation. As was the case with that other extinct species, the passenger pigeon, the tremendous loss of habitat resulting from the cutting of the vast eastern forests also served to concentrate the birds, making them more liable to losses through disease and shooting. The last specimen died in the Cincinnati Zoo in 1918.

27 MARCH 1728

Betwixt this plantation and Edenton there are many huckleberry slashes, which afford a convenient harbor for wolves and foxes. The first of these wild beasts is not so large and fierce as they are in other countries more northerly. He will not attack a man in the keenest of his hunger but run away from him, as from an animal more mischievous than himself. The foxes are much bolder and will sometimes not only make a stand but likewise assault anyone that would balk them of their prey. The inhabitants hereabouts take the trouble to dig abundance of wolf pits, so deep and perpendicular that when a wolf is once tempted into them he can no more scramble out again than a husband who has taken the leap can scramble out of matrimony. . . .

Within three or four miles of Edenton the soil appears to be a little more fertile, though it is much cut with slashes, which seem all to have a tendency toward the Dismal. This town is situate on the north side of Albemarle Sound, which is there about five miles over. A dirty slash runs all along the back of it, which

in the summer is a foul annoyance and furnishes abundance of
that Carolina plague, mosquitoes. There may be forty or fifty
houses, most of them small and built without expense. A citizen
here is counted extravagant if he has ambition enough to aspire
to a brick chimney. Justice herself is but indifferently lodged, the
courthouse having much of the air of a common tobacco house.
I believe this is the only metropolis in the Christian or Mahometan world where there is neither church, chapel, mosque,
synagogue, nor any other place of public worship of any sect or
religion whatsoever (*H* 206–7).

Wolves and foxes

The small wolves Byrd describes are red wolves *(Canis rufus),* native to the entire southeastern United States during the colonial period. Wolves were almost entirely exterminated from the whole area
by the early twentieth century, and by midcentury there was only a
remnant population in coastal Louisiana and Texas. A trapping and
captive-breeding program succeeded in saving the animal from total
extinction, but by the 1970s there were no red wolves left in the wild
anywhere in the United States.

In 1987 captive-born red wolves were reintroduced into the wild
in northeastern North Carolina, in the Alligator River National Wildlife Refuge and later in the Pocosin Lakes National Wildlife Refuge.
Wolves have also been reintroduced into the Smoky Mountains National Park, along the Tennessee–North Carolina border, but with less
success. The efforts to reestablish this predator in coastal North Carolina have been successful. Wolves are breeding in the wild, and there
are at this time as many as a hundred of the animals running free in the
refuges a little south of Byrd's line.

Red wolves are smaller than gray wolves, averaging around sixty
pounds, but are considerably larger and more heavily constructed than
coyotes. According to research by the U.S. Fish and Wildlife Service,
the repatriated red wolves in northeastern North Carolina feed mainly
on deer (50 percent of their diet), with raccoons and smaller mammals
making up most of the rest of their normal prey.

Byrd was probably right about the red wolf's reluctance to attack human beings, though lurid stories about wolf attacks in the Southeast persisted into the early nineteenth century. There are no recorded, well-documented instances of healthy red wolves attacking humans. Nevertheless, the wolves' habit of occasionally taking domestic animals did not endear them to settlers, and the trapping and killing of wolves was a common occurrence in the eighteenth century. John James Audubon, the famous illustrator of birds, wrote an account (reprinted in Clarence Ghodes, *Hunting in the Old South*) called the "Pitting of Wolves," which illustrates very well the attitude of early settlers toward the animals. Audubon's account, written in 1835, is full of examples of the wolves' damage to livestock. He adds, "Few instances have occurred among us of any attack made by Wolves on man, and only one has come under my own notice" (81). Audubon then relates the kind of hair-raising story—of a wolf pack attacking two men, killing and devouring one of them—that helped perpetuate the slaughter of wolves wherever they were found.

In later sections of both *The History* and *The Secret History*, Byrd describes red wolves as following the survey party constantly in order to feed on the party's leftovers. In return, he said, the wolves provided a nightly serenade. Anyone wishing to hear exactly the same kind of serenade Byrd listened to in 1728 might contact the refuge manager at the Alligator River National Wildlife Refuge. Nighttime trips to listen for wolves (the expeditions are called "wolf howlings") are conducted for limited groups on part of the refuge. The trips have become very popular, and it is not unusual now to find a fairly large group of enthusiasts gathering at one of the entrances to the refuge, talking excitedly, rubbing in liberal applications of insect repellent, and making plans to go howl with the wolves. Most nights, a group of human howlers will get a response from the animals. The refuge headquarters is located in the town of Manteo, North Carolina. The northern tip of the refuge itself is accessible off U.S. Highway 64, on the mainland of Dare County.

The foxes Byrd describes are almost certainly gray foxes *(Urocyon cinereoargenteus)*. Gray foxes prefer dense forests and tend to avoid the open farmland and fields where the red fox is more common. In the Southeast the gray was almost the only fox until large areas began to be cleared of woods, when the red fox began to move in. English emigrants in the South, coming from a fox-hunting tradition and being generally frustrated with the gray's reclusive tendencies (not to mention its catlike ability to climb trees) actually began importing red foxes from England, but this did not happen until later in the eighteenth century. The combination of forest clearing (which favored red foxes over grays) and the importation of an identical species of red fox from England made the latter *(Vulpes vulpes)* a more commonly seen animal. It is most likely, though, that the inhabitants of the "huckleberry slashes" and formidable thickets Byrd describes were gray foxes. Byrd's description of their boldness can most kindly be called an exaggeration. I have seen dozens of gray foxes in the last few years; they are shy, secretive creatures that I would not describe as "bold." I'll have to admit, though, that I never tried to "balk them of their prey."

Edenton

Byrd was not so critical of Edenton or of Carolinians in *The Secret History* as he was in the later work, when he was interested in promoting the interests of his own Virginia over those of the more southern colony. Edenton was founded in 1715 as "The Towne on Queene Anne's Creek" and was renamed in 1722 in honor of the governor, Charles Eden. Byrd was fairly accurate in describing the size of the town in 1728, but within only a few years of his survey the picture would change radically. Edenton became the most important port of the North Carolina colony as well as its civic and cultural center. By the 1740s and into the early eighteenth century, ships entering New Inlet would call at Edenton, and the town became a focal point of trade for the plantation economy along the Albemarle.

Today, Edenton is a picturesque little town with many buildings dating back to the middle and late 1700s. Construction of St. Paul's Episcopal Church was begun in 1736, the Cupola House was built in 1758, and the Barker House in 1782. (There was a St. Paul's Parrish in Edenton, on the shores of Albemarle Sound, as early as 1701, and services were held in a small wooden building. Byrd's comment about the utter absence of religion or houses of worship in the area was an exaggeration.) Since the town somehow escaped burning during the Civil War, it now offers a wealth of eighteenth-century and early nineteenth-century architectural examples to modern visitors.

Edenton sits at the end of a small bay on the Albemarle, which, as Byrd notes here, is about five miles across. The "dirty slash" he describes as running behind the town may be Pollock Swamp, a low-lying area to the north and west fed by several streams. Queen Anne Creek (earlier Queen Anne's Creek) lies to the east of town and is closer, but it is a rather scenic little body of water, lined with moss-laden cypress. Even William Byrd would not have described it as a "dirty slash."

28 MARCH 1728

While we were thus all hands uneasy, we were comforted with the news that this afternoon the line was finished through the Dismal. The messenger told us it had been the hard work of three days to measure the length of only five miles and mark the trees as they passed along; and by the most exact survey they found the breadth of the Dismal in this place to be completely fifteen miles. How wide it may be in other parts, we can give no account, but believe it grows narrower toward the north; possibly toward Albemarle Sound it may be something broader, where so many rivers issue out of it. All we know for certain is that from the place where the line entered the Dismal to where it came out we found the road round that portion of it which belongs to Virginia to be about sixty-five miles. How great the distance may be from each of those points round that part that falls within the bounds of Carolina we had no certain information, though 'tis conjectured it cannot be so little as thirty miles. At which rate the whole circuit must be about an hundred. What a mass of mud and dirt is treasured up within this filthy circumference, and what quantity of water must perpetually drain into it from the rising ground that surrounds it on every side!
(H 208–9)

"At which rate the whole circuit must be about an hundred"

Byrd's estimate of the size of the great swamp was probably very close to correct. Much of the land around the Great Dismal Swamp National Wildlife Refuge has been converted to agriculture, and small towns like South Mills and Corapeake (in North Carolina) and Deep Creek (in Virginia) lie just outside its boundaries. The city of Suffolk, Virginia, lies at the northernmost edge, and within the refuge itself is a network of canals and string-straight ditches that did not exist in the early eighteenth century. Outside the refuge, especially to the south, along the upper reaches of the Pasquotank River, there are long fingers of relatively undisturbed wilderness reaching back up toward the center of the swamp, but about two-thirds of what was in Byrd's day an uninhabited morass is now in agriculture, with intermittent fields breaking up the sections of forest and swamp.

30 MARCH 1728

The line was advanced this day six miles and thirty-five chains, the woods being pretty clear and interrupted with no swamp or other wet ground. The land hereabouts had all the marks of poverty, being for the most part sandy and full of pines. This kind of ground, though unfit for ordinary tillage, will however bring cotton and potatoes in plenty, and consequently food and raiment to such as are easily contented and, like the wild Irish, find more pleasure in laziness than luxury. It also makes a shift to produce Indian corn, rather by the felicity of the climate than the fertility of the soil. They who are more industrious than their neighbors may make what quantity of tar they please, though indeed they are not always sure of a market for it. The method of burning tar in Sweden and Muscovy succeeds not well in this warmer part of the world. It seems they kill the pine trees by barking them quite round at a certain height, which in those cold countries brings down the turpentine into the stump in a year's time. But experience has taught us that in warm climates the turpentine will not so easily descend but is either fixed in the upper parts of the tree or fried out by the intense heat of the sun (*H* 210–11).

"Sandy and full of pines"

Though Byrd could not have known it, he had come out of the low-lying swampland of the Dismal onto a fascinating topographic feature called the Suffolk Scarp. The scarp forms the western edge of the swamp, and it extends from north of Suffolk, Virginia, down to Newport, in Carteret County, North Carolina, approximately 150 miles to the south. It appears in satellite photographs as a very distinct white line (created by the sand Byrd describes) edging the perimeter of the lower ground to the east. The "sandy ridge" he mentions on his host's plantation near Edenton and the "poor sandy soil" he describes here are in a long, staggering line that was once a mainland beach, where ocean waves touched the land several hundred thousand years ago. All the land to the east of it, including not only the Dismal Swamp but also the farms, forests, and towns of eastern Virginia and North Carolina, was created during the ensuing centuries, as the rivers built up deposits of sand and soil.

2 APRIL 1728

In less than a mile from Somerton Creek the line was carried to Blackwater, which is the name of the upper part of Chowan, running some miles above the mouth of Nottoway. It must be observed that Chowan, after taking a compass round the most beautiful part of North Carolina, empties itself into Albemarle Sound a few miles above Edenton. The tide flows seven or eight miles higher than where the river changes its name and is navigable thus high for any small vessel. Our line intersected it exactly half a mile to the northward of the mouth of Nottoway. However, in obedience to His Majesty's command, we directed the surveyors to come down the river as far as the mouth of Nottoway in order to continue our true-west line from thence. Thus we found the mouth of Nottoway to be no more than half a minute farther to the northward than Mr. Lawson had formerly done. That gentleman's observation, it seems, placed it in 36 degrees 30 minutes, and our working made it out to be 36 degrees, 30 minutes and a half—a very inconsiderable variance.

In this camp three of the Meherrin Indians made us a visit.

They told us that the small remains of their nation had deserted
their ancient town, situated near the mouth of the Meherrin
River, for fear of the Catawba, who had killed fourteen of their
people the year before; and the few that survived that calamity
had taken refuge amongst the English on the east side of
Chowan. Though if the complaint of these Indians were true,
they are hardly used by our Carolina friends. But they are the
less to be pitied because they have ever been reputed the most
false and treacherous to the English of all the Indians in the
neighborhood (*H* 212–13).

Somerton Creek

There is still a Somerton, located about a half mile north of the
line. It is a crossroads on U.S. 13. There is also a Somerton Creek, and
just beyond that the Blackwater River. Byrd's attempt to abide by both
earlier directives—that the line be on or about the parallel of 36 degrees and 30 minutes and that it run though "the mouth of Weyanoke
Creek," which he took to be the point where the Nottoway and the
Blackwater converge to form the Chowan—resulted in his dropping
the line about a half mile to the south, then continuing in a westerly
course. The actual latitude of the line just before it touches the Blackwater, according to National Coast and Geodetic Survey maps and
satellite measurement, is right at 36°33′ N. Byrd's correction, then, was
very close, especially considering the instrumentation available in 1728.
(The sextant was not invented until 1731—three years after the survey.
The surveyors could have used only a compass, an astrolabe, a spirit
level, measuring chains, timepieces, and reference books giving the
angles of declination for heavenly bodies at specific times of the year.)

Meherrin Indians

Byrd mentions several tribes in his accounts, including the
Catawba, the Meherrin, the Tuscarora, the Cherokee, the Saponi/
Occaneechee, the Sauro, and the Nottoway. Many small tribes living
in the Carolinas and Virginia in the early eighteenth century virtually
disappeared during the fighting between Native Americans and colonists that went on sporadically between 1710 and 1760. Other small

groups were assimilated into larger groups. Intertribal rivalries and ha-
treds, disease (especially smallpox), and the abuse of alcohol decimated
the tribes when they were not actually fighting against the English.

The Meherrins were of the same linguistic group as the Tuscaroras,
the Nottoways, the Cherokees, and the tribes of the Iroquois Confederacy in New York and Canada. They had been allies of their cousins
and close neighbors, the Tuscaroras, during the bloody Tuscarora war
of 1711–13, and by 1728 they were down to a remnant of their former
strength. That conflict was settled with the help of militia from South
Carolina and about five hundred Catawba warriors.

The Catawbas, of Siouan stock, were enemies of the Tuscaroras
and other Iroquoian groups, and they found themselves allied with the
English in both North and South Carolina during uprisings by other
native peoples. The Catawbas needed guns, and the white settlers
needed powerful allies.

The Meherrins remain today as a tribe with state recognition in
a few northeastern counties in North Carolina. There are now about
six hundred Meherrins in several small communities in counties near
the Chowan River. The Catawbas survive as a tribe with federal recognition and a reservation in South Carolina. Many of the Tuscaroras
left alive and not sold into slavery after the Tuscarora war left North
Carolina and Virginia and joined the other members of the Iroquois
Federation.

5 APRIL 1728

> Because the spring was now pretty forward and the rattlesnakes
> began to crawl out of their winter quarters and might grow
> dangerous both to the men and their horses, it was determined
> to proceed no farther with the line until next fall. Besides, the
> uncommon fatigue the people had undergone for near six weeks
> together and the inclination they all had to visit their respective
> families made a recess highly reasonable (*H* 216).

Rattlesnakes

Byrd was apparently fascinated by rattlesnakes, but he mentions
no other snakes of any kind in either of his accounts. The snakes he

describes here and elsewhere are specimens of the timber rattlesnake, *Crotalus horridus,* which can reach a length of over six feet, with an impressive girth. Though absent now from many of the areas where Bryd reported seeing them, they once were widely distributed throughout both states. They can still be found in the mountains of North Carolina and Virginia as well as in low-lying areas where there is comparatively little human disturbance, such as around the Dismal Swamp. See also the comments on Byrd's observations of rattlesnakes on 26 September, below.

7 April 1728

In the morning we dispatched a runner to the Nottoway town to let the Indians know we intended them a visit that evening, and our honest landlord was so kind as to be our pilot thither, being about four miles from his house. Accordingly, in the afternoon we marched in good order to the town, where the female scouts, stationed on an eminence for that purpose, had no sooner spied us but they gave notice of our approach to their fellow citizens by continual whoops and cries, which could not possibly have been more dismal at the sight of their most implacable enemies. This signal assembled all their great men, who received us in a body and conducted us into the fort. . . .

The young men had painted themselves in a hideous manner, not so much for ornament as terror. In that frightful equipage they entertained us with sundry war dances, wherein they endeavored to look as formidable as possible. The instrument they danced to was an Indian drum, that is, a large gourd with a skin braced taut over the mouth of it. . . .

Upon this occasion the ladies had arrayed themselves in all their finery. They were wrapped in their red and blue matchcoats, thrown so negligently about them that their mahogany skins appeared in several parts, like the Lacedaemonian damsels of old. Their hair was braided with white and blue peak and hung gracefully in a large roll upon their shoulders.

This peak consists of small cylinders cut out of a conch shell, drilled through and strung like beads. It serves them both for money and jewels, the blue being of much greater value than the white for the same reason that Ethiopian mistresses in France are dearer than French, because they are more scarce. The women wear necklaces and bracelets of these precious materials when they have a mind to appear lovely. Though their complexions be a little sad-colored, yet their shapes are very straight and well proportioned. Their faces are seldom handsome, yet they have an air of innocence and bashfulness that with a little less dirt would not fail to make them desirable. Such charms might have had their full effect upon men who had been so long deprived of female conversation but that the whole winter's soil was so crusted on the skins of those dark angels that it required a very strong appetite to approach them. The bear's oil with which they anoint their persons all over makes their skins soft and at the same time protects them from every species of vermin that use to be troublesome to other uncleanly people (*H* 217–18).

Peak

This combination of currency and costume jewelry has already been described. Interestingly, it was used not just by coastal and lowland tribes but by native people as far away as the mountains, who traded for it. Byrd's comment on the relative value of "blue" versus white peak is in line with Rountree's description of the nature and value of the material: "Peak was made from quahog *(Venus mercenaria)* shells and came in white or dark purple ('black') forms. . . . The purple peak, known to later writers as wampum peak, was more valuable because of the lesser area of the shell with that color" (72–73). Byrd here repeats his earlier (and erroneous) assertion that the beads were made of conch rather than clamshells. Rountree has a lengthy description of all aspects of Powhatan attire, including clothing, necklaces, bracelets, earrings, headgear, tattooing, and painting (60–78). For a discussion of the various kinds of beads used as ornamentation and trade items, see also Ben C. McCary (28–30).

Bear's oil

The black bear *(Ursus americanus)* was an extremely useful animal as well as an important symbol for Native Americans in the Southeast. Byrd's party depended heavily on the meat of bears during their fall expedition, and they found great numbers of the animals along certain portions of their journey. The description given here of bear's oil as an insect repellent is similar to those given in other accounts written in the eighteenth century and earlier. Thomas Harriot, in the 1580s, described the natives of Roanoke Island and the surrounding mainland as using the fat or oil of bears in order to keep away biting insects.

8 APRIL 1728

We rested on our clean mats very comfortably, though alone, and the next morning went to the toilet of some of the Indian ladies, where, what with the charms of their persons and the smoke of their apartments, we were almost blinded. They offered to give us silk-grass baskets of their own making, which we modestly refused, knowing that an Indian present, like that of a nun, is a liberality put out to interest and a bribe placed to the greatest advantage. Our chaplain observed with some concern that the ruffles of our fellow travelers were a little discolored with puccoon, wherewith the good man had been told those ladies used to improve their invisible charms (*H* 222).

Puccoon

Puccoon is a red dye made of either the bloodroot *(Sanguinaria canadensis)*—which is sometimes called "red puccoon" and "Indian paint"—or of a plant that is still called "puccoon," *Lithospermum caroliniense.* Charles F. Millspaugh (83–84) and McCary (32) discuss the use of the bloodroot as a dye and body paint, but Rountree makes a convincing case that *Lithospermum caroliniense,* known to the Powhatans for both "its rarity and its beauty when made into body paint," was the more likely of the two. Bloodroot was more often used for decorating shields and other implements (76). The puccoon dye was used as a sort of body rouge; it rubbed off on English linen quite easily, as Byrd's men discovered.

In some ways Byrd seems enlightened in his attitudes toward the Indians and their treatment by the whites. He is saddened by the diminishment of the Nottoways ("the only Indians of any consequence now remaining within the limits of Virginia"), and he acknowledges that the rum "too liberally supplied by the English that live near them" has been a major contributor to their losses.

Byrd's tolerant attitude toward racial intermarriage (an attitude he sometimes expresses jokingly, sometimes seriously) also seems out of place, coming from the pen of an eighteenth-century gentleman. He wonders why settlers have not more often taken Indian wives, adding, "I may safely venture to say, the Indian women would have made altogether as honest wives for the first planters as they used to purchase from aboard the ships. 'Tis strange, therefore, that any good Christian should have refused a wholesome, straight bedfellow, when he might have had so fair a portion with her as the merit of saving her soul" (*H* 222). However, as his comments later about the French and their success in forming strong alliances with the Indians make clear, his tongue-in-cheek advice to take Indian wives has political motivations. Byrd was worried about the safety of the English colonies from attack by the French and their Indian allies.

In *The Secret History,* Byrd is less equivocal in his observations of the travelers' sexual relations with the Nottoway women, noting that Meanwell's (that is, William Dandridge's) "curiosity made him try the difference between them and other women, to the disobligation of his ruffles, which betrayed what he had been doing." He adds in the same section, "I could discern by some of our gentlemen's linen, discolored by the soil of the Indian ladies, that they had been convincing themselves in the point of their having no fur" (*SH* 82).

2 ✤ EARLY FALL

The Meherrin to the Roanoke and the Dan

BY THE TIME the group disbanded in April, the line had been drawn a little over seventy-three miles from its starting point at Currituck Inlet. On 20 September the North Carolina party and the Virginia party met close to the place where they had stopped in the spring, near the Meherrin River, to resume the survey.

The first day was spent largely in checking the provisions brought by both parties, which included not only food but also a sufficient quantity of powder and ball. Since they were leaving civilization behind them, the party had to be self-reliant, providing its own food and its own protection as it made its way westward. Byrd points out that the proposed route would carry them across "the path which the northern Indians pass to make war upon the Catawbas and shall go through the very woods that are frequented by those straggling savages, who commit so many murders upon our frontiers" (*SH* 90). The "northern Indians," of course, were transplanted Tuscaroras and other Iroquoian Confederacy tribes, who had not forgotten the Catawbas' contribution to their defeat in the war of 1711–13. (See the discussion of tribes in chapter 1.) Most of the territory beyond the Meherrin River and lying close to the line was still without white inhabitants in 1728, though trading parties and other groups of explorers traveled through it. Byrd explains that "because there was much work to be done and some danger from the Indians in the uninhabited part of the country, it was necessary to provide a competent number of men.

Accordingly, seventeen able hands were listed on the part of Virginia, who were most of them Indian traders and expert woodsmen" (*H* 171).

Byrd seems thoroughly fascinated by the profusion of plant and animal species encountered along this section of his route. He describes various plants he believes are efficacious in treating lung, heart, and stomach disorders; administers herbal medicines (concocted along the march) to any of his men who might have the temerity to complain about illness or injury; and waxes eloquent on the subject of herbal treatments for rattlesnake bites. (Fortunately, no one was bitten on the trip, and so the power of such treatments remained untested.) Among the animals and birds he mentions are deer, bears, beavers, buffalo, wildcats, panthers, turkeys, and cranes.

Today, U.S. 58 and 158 parallel this section of Byrd's line on the north and south, respectively, at a distance of from five to twenty miles. The boundary line is cut by Interstates 95 and 85 as well as by other major north-south highways such as U.S. 15, 301, and 501. A fairly large expanse of the land Byrd describes in this section is now underwater. The Roanoke River was dammed in 1950 to form Kerr Reservoir, a vast, sprawling, multiarmed body of water covering some fifty thousand acres, with 800 miles of shoreline along the Virginia–North Carolina border. A few years later, Lake Gaston's twenty thousand acres of water, with 350 miles of shoreline, drowned an additional 35-mile-long section of the Roanoke. Combined, the two lakes flood a stretch of the Roanoke near Byrd's original survey line about 42 miles long.

On either end of the great reservoirs, the huge forests of oak, hickory, and chestnut trees have given way to farming country—patchwork-quilt patterns of fields and pastures, broken by smaller or larger tracts of woods and swamps. In Occoneechee State Park and Staunton River State Park (both of them a little north of the state line) and in the Kerr Lake Recreation Area, on the North Carolina side, visitors can see fairly large tracts of mature forests—though without the chestnut trees. Some of the private land on both sides of the line is also heavily wooded, but an aerial view of the countryside shows the tracts of woods surrounded by farms. Several small to medium-sized towns, including Emporia, South Hill, Clarksville, and South Boston (on the

Virginia side) and Roanoke Rapids, Henderson, Oxford, and Roxboro
(on the North Carolina side) flank the line. Byrd first crossed the Dan
River a little east of present-day Danville, Virginia, and almost at the
town limits of Milton, North Carolina, on 10 October 1728. At that
point the party was twenty-one days and approximately sixty-two
miles from the last white settlement.

The deer and turkeys Byrd describes remain in large numbers,
but bears are infrequent visitors to this area now (usually making their
way up the river-bottom corridors from eastern North Carolina or occasionally straying down from the mountains of Virginia). The buffalo
and panthers, of course, disappeared long ago. Even the chestnut forests
are gone, victims of an imported disease that blighted American chestnut trees in the early twentieth century.

This segment of Byrd's survey carried the men beyond the coastal
plain and into the Piedmont section of North Carolina and Virginia,
and he comments on the rockiness of the soil and the rise in elevation
near the "first falls of the Roanoke," at present-day Roanoke Rapids,
North Carolina. The piedmont soil nourished a different kind of vegetation, and Byrd writes at great length on both the plants and the animals in this region. Many of the plants he describes have medicinal
applications, and he comments on the efficacy of certain snakebite
remedies made from star grass *(Aletris farinosa)*, St. Andrew's cross *(Hypericum hypericoides)*, and rattlesnake fern *(Botrychium virginianum)*—all
of which can still be found in the area. He made "vomits" and "purges"
out of wild ipecac *(Euphorbia ipecacuanha;* also called "Carolina ipecac")
and treated fevers with tea made from dogwood bark.

Since this segment of the journey took the party farther from white
settlements, they found a greater abundance of large animals than
they had previously encountered. The wolves Byrd had mentioned
earlier become constant followers now, and he writes with growing fre-
quency of bears and panthers as well as deer. The men encountered
their first buffalo just south and west of what is now Clarksville, Virginia, prompting the first of several entries Byrd makes describing the
great animals and speculating on their habits and even their possible
domestication and use by colonists.

19 SEPTEMBER 1728

About ten this morning we wished health to Sally and her family and forded over Nottoway River at Bolton's Ferry, the water being very low. We called upon Samuel Kindred again, who regaled us with a beefsteak and our men with cider. Here we had like to have listed a mulatto wench for cook to the expedition, who formerly lived with Colonel Ludwell. After halting here about an hour, we pursued our journey, and in the way Richard Smith showed me the star root, which infallibly cures the bite of the rattlesnake.

Nine miles from thence we forded over Meherrin River near Mr. Kinchen's, believing we should be at the place of meeting before the rest of the commissioners (*SH* 94).

Star root

Louis B. Wright correctly identifies this as star grass or colicroot *(Aletris farinosa),* a small plant with whitish or yellowish leaves. Stargrass roots were used in medicines to treat stomach disorders. Foster and Duke cite the plant's use in treatments for indigestion, diarrhea, rheumatism, and jaundice. Millspaugh describes a tincture made from the roots as being extremely bitter and notes that it was used in a tonic to treat colic and rheumatism, among other ailments. Star grass is found fairly frequently in "moist habitats in woods, meadows, and savannahs" throughout the area (Radford et al., *Atlas,* 117). Nothing in the plant would make it likely to be an effective antidote to snake venom.

21 SEPTEMBER 1728

We dispatched away the surveyors without the loss of time, who, with all their diligence, could carry the line no farther than 3 miles and 176 poles, by reason the low ground was one entire thicket. In that distance they crossed the Meherrin River the fourth time.

22 SEPTEMBER 1728

Several of our men had intermitting fevers but were soon restored to their health again by proper remedies. Our chief medicine was dogwood bark, which we used, instead of that of Peru, with good success. Indeed, it was given in large quantity, but then, to make the patients amends, they swallowed much fewer doses (*H* 224–25).

Dogwood

Foster and Duke point out that the very common flowering dogwood *(Cornus florida)* has a long history of medicinal use. A tea made from the root bark was used as a substitute for quinine in treating malarial fevers. Dogwood is one of the most common and among the most easily recognizable of all the low-growing trees in the southern woodlands. The fruit of the tree, in the form of red "dogwood berries," is also a valuable food for wildlife.

23 SEPTEMBER 1728

The surveyors came to us at night, though they had not brought the line so far as our camp, for which reason we thought it needless to go forward till they came up with us. They could run no more than four miles and five poles, because the ground was everywhere grown up with thick bushes. The soil here appeared to be very good, though much broken betwixt Fontaine Creek and Roanoke River. The line crossed the Meherrin the fifth and last time; nor were our people sorry to part with a stream the meanders of which had given them so much trouble.

Our hunters brought us four wild turkeys, which at that season began to be fat and very delicious, especially the hens. These birds seem to be of the bustard kind and fly heavily. Some of them are exceedingly large and weigh upwards of forty pounds; nay, some bold historians venture to say upwards of fifty. They run very fast, stretching forth their wings all the time, like the ostrich, by way of sails to quicken their speed. They roost commonly upon very high trees, standing near some river or creek, and are so stupefied at the sight of fire that, if you make a blaze in the night near the place where they roost, you may fire upon them several times successively before they will dare to fly away. Their spurs are so sharp and strong that the

Indians used formerly to point their arrows with them, though now they point them with a sharp white stone. In the spring the turkey cocks begin to gobble, which is the language wherein they make love (*H* 225–26).

Wild turkeys

Wild turkeys *(Meleagris gallopavo)* are still common along both sides of the line. By the end of the nineteenth century, turkey numbers were very low, but restoration and restocking efforts in the early and mid-twentieth centuries have brought back the magnificent birds in great numbers. The turkey, like the white-tailed deer, is a remarkable success story for modern wildlife management. In the middle of the twentieth century, the entire North American population of the big birds was only around five hundred thousand. By 1995 that number had increased to well over four million, according to the National Wild Turkey Federation, and the population has continued to expand rapidly since that time.

Byrd cites both fact and fiction regarding the wild turkey here. Generally he is correct, but he exaggerates the maximum size of the bird. A turkey weighing much over twenty pounds must be considered very large, and one weighing over twenty-five pounds would be extremely unusual. Still, a twenty-pound bird is an impressive animal, and Byrd would certainly not be the first woodsman to overestimate the size of a mature wild turkey. After all, a big male turkey (a tom) is easily twice as big as a Canada goose, and to see one or more of them walking through the woods or suddenly taking flight is an impressive sight.

Byrd is correct about their roosting in tall trees, their preference for roosting "near some river or creek," and their ability to run swiftly with their wings spread out. The spurs of an adult male turkey are formidable weapons. They are very hard, very sharp, two inches long or more in large males, and I suppose they could conceivably be used as arrow points. Other early writers, including John Smith, also said that turkey spurs were used to tip arrows. (See also the entry and comments on wild turkeys for 26 October, below.)

Turkeys are capable of making a wide variety of sounds, from chickenlike clucking noises to what sound like purrs and barely audible chirps, but the call familiar to most people (and the only one Byrd mentions) is the gobble of the male in the springtime. As Byrd notes, it "is the language wherein they make love." Male (or tom) turkeys announce their presence to females by strutting with fanned-out tails and gobbling loudly. The sound of the hen during mating season is typically a soft clucking noise. Hunters locate the gobblers by sound, then try to lure the turkeys into shotgun range by imitating the clucking of a receptive hen. Both Virginia and North Carolina have controlled seasons on the big birds during the spring mating season, with strict limits on numbers taken. Only males are legal game during the spring season. Interestingly, the part of the line that Byrd surveyed in the early fall of 1728, from the Meherrin River to the Dan, once again has some of the highest turkey populations in either state, thanks to good habitat and the restocking and management efforts begun in the mid-twentieth century.

24 SEPTEMBER 1728

This part of the country being very proper for raising cattle and hogs, we observed the inhabitants lived in great plenty without killing themselves with labor. I found near our camp some plants of that kind of rattlesnake root called star grass. The leaves shoot out circularly and grow horizontally and near the ground. The root is in shape not unlike the rattle of that serpent and is a strong antidote against the bite of it. It is very bitter and where it meets with any poison works with violent sweats, but where it meets with none has no sensible operation but that of putting the spirits into a great hurry and so of promoting perspiration. The rattlesnake hath an utter antipathy to this plant, insomuch that if you smear your hands with the juice of it, you may handle the viper safely. Thus much I can say on my own experience: that once in July, when these snakes are in their greatest vigor, I besmeared a dog's nose with the powder of this root and made him trample on a large rattlesnake several times, which, however, was so far from biting him that it perfectly sickened at the dog's approach and turned its head from him with the utmost aversion (*H* 226–27).

"That kind of rattlesnake root called star grass"

Presumably this is the same plant referred to in *The Secret History* in the entry for 19 September. It is a member of the lily family. Byrd's description here, of leaves lying in a circular formation near the ground, certainly fits the star grass *(A. farinosa),* as does his comment about the bitterness of the plant. His faith in the curative qualities of the plant for snakebite, however, is unfounded. It is also difficult to imagine that a rattlesnake would have an "utter antipathy" to the little plant, to such an extent that it would refuse to bite a man or dog anointed with a powder made from the roots. Star grass is still sometimes used in folk medicine, but usually as a treatment for indigestion.

Byrd's observation that the root of the plant "is in shape not unlike the rattle of that serpent and is a strong antidote against the bite of it" may reflect a belief in the "doctrine of signatures," a very old idea about the efficacy of certain plants. According to the doctrine of signatures, a plant that was shaped like or in some way resembled a particular part of the body might be useful in treating problems associated with that body part. Thus the sharp-lobed hepatica, also called liver leaf, was thought to be useful in treating liver disease because of a fancied resemblance between its leaves and the human liver.

25 SEPTEMBER 1728

The surveyors, taking the advantage of clear woods, pushed on the line seven miles and forty poles. In the meantime the commissioners marched with the baggage about twelve miles and took up their quarters near the banks of the Beaver Pond (which is one branch of Fontaine Creek), just by the place where the surveyors were to finish their day's work. In our march one of them men killed a small rattlesnake, which had no more than two rattles. Those vipers remain in vigor generally until the end of September, or sometimes later if the weather continue a little warm. On this consideration we had provided three several sorts of rattlesnake root, made up into proper doses and ready for immediate use, in case any one of the men or their horses had been bitten. We crossed Fontaine Creek once more in our journey this day and found the grounds very rich, notwithstanding they were broken and stony (*H* 227).

Clear woods

Much of the land around the Meherrin River, where it crosses the dividing line, was (and still is) low, swampy, and overgrown with thick brush. Byrd had already commented that progress along the Meherrin, through a vast tangle of low thickets and swamps, was excruciatingly slow. Beyond Fontaine Creek and toward Beaverdam Creek, in present-day Greensville County, Virginia, the land begins to rise. This is the beginning of the Piedmont section of Virginia and North Carolina, and the relatively flat coastal plain begins to give way to rolling hills. Here the land is sometimes rocky, since the soil lies more thinly on bedrock than does the soil in the coastal plain. Interstate 95, as it drops south from Emporia, Virginia, crosses the line and heads toward Roanoke Rapids, runs more or less along the dividing line between the coastal plain and the Piedmont. As Byrd notes a few days later, the Roanoke was navigable from the sea up to "the first falls of the Roanoke" (present-day Roanoke Rapids, where Interstate 95 crosses the river). Most important for Byrd, the men are leaving the difficult swamps behind and moving through relatively open forests.

26 SEPTEMBER 1728

We hurried away the surveyors without loss of time, who extended the line 10 miles and 60 poles, the grounds proving dry and free from underwoods. By the way the chain carriers killed two more rattlesnakes, which I own was a little ungrateful, because two or three of the men had strided over them without receiving any hurt, though one of these vipers had made bold to strike at one of the baggage horses as he went along, but by good luck his teeth only grazed on the hoof without doing him any damage. However, these accidents were, I think, so many arguments that we had very good reason to defer our coming out till the twentieth of September. We observed abundance of St-Andrew's-cross in all the woods we passed through, which is the common remedy used by the Indian traders to cure their horses when they are bitten by rattlesnakes. It grows on a straight stem about eighteen inches high and bears a yellow flower on the top that has an eye of black in the middle, with several pairs of narrow leaves shooting out at right angles from the stock over against one another. This antidote grows providentially all over the woods and upon all sorts of soil, that it may be everywhere at hand in case disaster should happen, and may be had all the hot months while the snakes are dangerous.

About four o'clock in the afternoon we took up our quarters upon Cabin Branch, which also discharges itself into Fontaine Creek. On our way we observed several meadows clothed with very rank grass and branches full of tall reeds, in which cattle keep themselves fat good part of the winter. But hogs are as injurious to both as goats are said to be to vines, and for that reason it was not lawful to sacrifice them to Bacchus. We halted by the way to christen two children at a spring, where their mothers waylaid us for that good purpose (*H* 227–28).

"Two more rattlesnakes"

Here, as before, Byrd is referring to the timber rattlesnake, as the somewhat larger eastern diamondback is not found much above the 35th parallel in North Carolina and the pygmy rattlesnake not above the 36th (and then only in the easternmost counties). Rattlesnakes are rare in the Piedmont at the present time, though they are fairly common in some areas of the mountains of both states. A lowland version of the timber rattlesnake, the canebrake rattlesnake *(Crotalus horridus atricaudatus)* occurs on both sides of the line, but more frequently in Carolina than in Virginia and usually in the eastern section. Herpetologists disagree as to whether the canebrake rattlesnake is taxonomically different enough to be regarded as a subspecies. In both North

Carolina and Virginia, the canebrake/timber rattlesnake is now a protected species.

St.-Andrew's-cross

This common plant *(Hypericum hypericoides)* is a member of the St.-John's-wort family, and as such has been used for centuries in herbal medicines. It is widely distributed, growing in sandy soil in most of the eastern United States. Byrd is correct in suggesting that the Indians set much store by the St.-Andrew's-cross. Native Americans chewed the root of the plant as a remedy for snakebite. They also used a root tea for colic, fevers, toothaches, and diarrhea. It was occasionally used for skin problems. Like St.-John's-wort, it contains hypericin and may cause photodermatitis (skin burns) in sensitive persons exposed to the sun (Foster and Duke 92, 114). In *The Secret History* Byrd also mentions seeing specimens of the "fern rattlesnake root" (probably the rattlesnake fern, *Botrychinium virginianum*) on 26 September. This is a very common fern occurring in rich hardwood forests all over the southeast as well as in other sections of the country. Like the St.-Andrew's-cross, it was commonly used by Native Americans for a variety of ailments, including snakebite.

27 SEPTEMBER 1728

We crossed over Pea Creek about four miles from our quarters and three miles farther Lizard Creek, both of which empty their waters into Roanoke River. . . . We proceeded as far as Pigeon Roost Creek, which also runs into Roanoke, and there quartered.

In the stony grounds we rode over we found great quantity of the true ipecacuanha, which in this part of the world is called Indian physic. This has several stalks growing up from the same root about a foot high, bearing a leaf resembling that of a strawberry. It is not so strong as that from Brazil but has the same happy effects if taken in somewhat a larger dose. It is an excellent vomit and generally cures intermitting fevers and bloody fluxes at once or twice taking. There is abundance of it in the upper part of the country, where it delights most in a stony soil intermixed with black mold (H 228).

Pigeon Roost Creek

The creek was named after the large numbers of passenger pigeons (now extinct) that roosted there. (See the discussion of passenger pigeons after the entry for 19 October, below.)

Ipecacuanha

Byrd here describes wild ipecac *(Euphorbia ipecacuanha)*, another plant with a long history of use in folk medicines. Merritt Lyndon Fernald, in *Gray's Manual of Botany,* notes that the plant has very strong emetic properties, just as the Brazilian version does (969). The emetic qualities are in the root tea; a tea made from the leaves was sometimes used for treating diabetes. The root extract is an extremely powerful laxative, and juice from the plant can actually cause blistering.

Byrd refers to various purges and emetics on his journeys. Like many eighteenth-century practitioners of medicine—whether professional or amateur—he tended to regard most illnesses and bodily disorders as coming from some sort of excess. Therefore, he prescribed—and apparently forcefully administered at times—"vomits" and laxatives for gout, bruises, headaches, fevers, and all sorts of stomach disorders. Nobody on the journey died.

The practice of administering strong laxatives to cure a wide variety of ailments persisted, especially in rural areas, well into the twentieth century. Near where I live now (which happens to be almost where Byrd first crossed the Dan River in October 1728), there lived in the 1950s a specialist in home remedies who called himself a "conjure doctor." According to older residents in the community, patients came from as far away as Washington, D.C., and New York to be cured. The conjure doctor's chief and perhaps his only medicine (as far as I could gather in conversation) was Epsom salt (hydrated magnesium sulfate)—an extremely powerful cathartic that he had shipped in by the barrel. Other rural remedies relied on some of the same plants Byrd mentions and on some he does not mention, such as pokeweed. The effect on the patient was invariably the same. Byrd would no doubt have been pleased.

28 SEPTEMBER 1728

The great falls of the Roanoke lie about twenty miles lower, to which a sloop of moderate burden may come up. There are, besides these, many smaller falls above, though none that entirely intercept the passage of the river, as the great ones do by a chain of rocks for eight miles together. The river forks about thirty-six miles higher, and both branches are pretty equal in breadth where they divide, though the southern, now called the Dan, runs up the farthest. That to the north runs away near northwest and is called the Staunton, and heads not far from the source of the Appomatox River, while the Dan stretches away pretty near west and runs clear through the great mountains. . . .

We proceeded to the canoe landing on Roanoke, where we passed the river with the baggage. But the horses were directed to a ford about a mile higher, called by the Indians Monissep, which signifies in their jargon "shallow water." This is the ford where the Indian traders used to cross with their horses in the way to the Catawba nation. There are many rocks in the river thereabouts, on which grows a kind of water grass, which the wild geese are fond of and resort to it in great numbers. . . .

By the way one of our men killed another rattlesnake with eleven rattles, having a large gray squirrel in his maw, the head of which was already digested while the body remained still entire. The way these snakes catch their prey is thus: they ogle the poor little animal till by force of the charm he falls down stupefied and senseless on the ground. In that condition the snake approaches and moistens first one ear and then the other with his sprawl, and after that is done, he draws this member into his mouth and after it, by slow degrees, all the rest of the body (*H* 229–30).

Great Falls of the Roanoke

Byrd refers to the rapids on the Roanoke River near present-day Roanoke Rapids and Weldon, North Carolina, a little south of the line. East and south of Weldon, the river runs through Carolina's coastal plain; the falls mark the edge of the Piedmont. Interstate 95 crosses the

Roanoke at the "great falls" Byrd describes. The river was navigable, as he points out, up to these rapids.

"A kind of water grass, which the wild geese are fond of"

The area of the Roanoke that Byrd describes throughout much of this section is flooded by Gaston and Kerr Reservoirs. In this paragraph, he is referring to a point downstream from the enormous Kerr Reservoir dam, at the upper end of Lake Gaston. It so happens that there is a major wildlife-management area near here, Elm Hill, and large numbers of wintering ducks and geese still gather at this point to feed in the shallows. The wildlife-management area is accessible off U.S. 1, which crosses the upper end of Lake Gaston just below the Elm Hill area and drops into North Carolina less than five miles further south. Many species of ducks, as well as Canada geese *(Branta canadensis)* and sometimes tundra swans *(Cygnus columbianus),* use the Roanoke River basin as a migratory route into eastern North Carolina. With the formation of the great reservoirs, many of them now winter on Kerr and Gaston, especially around the Elm Hill Refuge.

"The way these snakes catch their prey"

Byrd here merely repeats an old superstition about snakes "charming" their prey. The real manner of their hunting is not nearly so mysterious. The rattlesnake approaches very stealthily or lies in ambush, waiting for his victim. He strikes, injecting a fatal dose of venom, then releases it. The squirrel or other small mammal runs off, but it will not run far before the hemotoxin begins to take effect. The snake, meanwhile, follows the trail of the wounded animal by smell, using sensory glands in its forked tongue. By the time it arrives the prey animal is usually dead, and the hemotoxin, which works by breaking down the walls of the blood vessels, has even begun to predigest the snake's intended dinner. Swallowing the animal is a matter of the snake's dislocating its hinged jaws and literally crawling over the prey.

Reports of such "charming" are widespread, and they may have come from observations of stricken animals. A small mammal that has been bitten by a rattlesnake may be still alive but almost unable to move by the time the snake arrives. Anyone seeing the snake glide up

to the animal, wait patiently for it to fall paralyzed or dead by the hemotoxin, then begin to swallow it might naturally assume that the
snake had hypnotized its prey.

29 SEPTEMBER 1728

We found in the low ground several plants of the fern root,
which is said to be much the strongest antidote yet discovered
against the poison of the rattlesnake. The leaves of it resemble
those of the fern, from whence it derives its name. Several stalks
shoot from the same root, about six inches long, that lie mostly
on the ground. It grows in a very rich soil, under the protection
of some tall tree that shades it from the meridian beams of the
sun. The root has a faint spicy taste and is preferred by the
southern Indians to all other counterpoisons in this country. But
there is another sort preferred by the northern Indians that they
call Seneca rattlesnake root, to which wonderful virtues are as-
cribed in the cure of pleurisies, fevers, rheumatisms, and drop-
sies, besides it being a powerful antidote against the venom of
the rattlesnake.

In the evening the messenger we had sent to Christanna returned with five Saponi Indians. We could not entirely rely on
the dexterity of our own men, which induced us to send for
some of the Indians. We agreed with two of the most expert of
them upon reasonable terms to hunt for us the remaining part
of our expedition. But one of them falling sick soon after, we
were content to take only the other, whose hunting name was
Bearskin. This Indian, either by his skill or good luck, supplied
us plentifully all the way with meat, seldom discharging his
piece in vain. By his assistance, therefore, we were able to keep
our men to their business, without suffering them to straggle
about the woods on pretense of furnishing us with necessary
food (*H* 231).

Fern root

Probably Byrd refers to the rattlesnake fern *(Botrychium virginianum)*. This is a small fern with fleshy roots growing in deciduous

woods all along both sides of the line. It is still very common, especially in the Piedmont and lower mountains.

Seneca rattlesnake root

This herb *(Polygala senega)* is commonly called Seneca snakeroot and, like the fern root, served colonial Americans in a variety of remedies. According to Radford et al. (*Guide* 216), Seneca rattlesnake root grows well in limestone soil in the mountains of Virginia and North Carolina, but the plant occurs only occasionally along Byrd's line (Harvill 137). Byrd does not mention actually seeing a specimen.

Saponi Indians

The Saponi Indians were given a trading fort, Fort Christanna, in Brunswick County, Virginia, in 1713. Originally, the Saponis and their near relatives the Occaneechis had controlled trade routes through much of this section of Piedmont Virginia. The tribe now has state recognition (from North Carolina but not from Virginia), with most of its members living near Hillsborough, North Carolina.

The Indian hunter Byrd mentions here contributed to the writer's understanding of Native American religious traditions. Just at the outskirts of the city of Danville, Virginia, a marker designates the spot at which Bearskin instructed William Byrd in the essentials of Saponi religion, which Byrd duly recorded in *The History*. (See the comments on Byrd's discussion with Bearskin in the entry dated 13 October, below.)

30 SEPTEMBER 1728

It had rained all night and made everything so wet that our surveyors could not get to their work before noon. They could therefore measure no more than 4 miles and 220 poles, which, according to the best information we could get, was near as high as the uppermost inhabitant at that time.

We crossed the Indian trading path above-mentioned about a mile from our camp and a mile beyond that forded Hawtree Creek. The woods we passed through had all the tokens of sterility, except a small poisoned field on which grew no tree bigger than a slender sapling. The larger trees had been

destroyed either by fire or caterpillar, which is often the case in
the upland woods, and the places where such desolation happens
are often called poisoned fields. We took up our quarters upon a
branch of Great Creek, where there was tolerable good grass for
the poor horses. These poor animals, having now got beyond
the latitude of corn, were obliged to shift as well as they could
for themselves.

On our way the men roused a bear, which being the first we
had seen since we came out, the poor beast had many pursuers.
Several persons contended for the credit of killing him, though
he was so poor he was not worth the powder. This was some
disappointment to our woodsmen, who commonly prefer the
flesh of bears to every kind of venison. There is something indeed peculiar to this animal, namely, that its fat is very firm and
may be eaten plentifully without rising in the stomach. The paw
(which when stripped of the hair looks like a human foot) is accounted a delicious morsel by all who are not shocked at the un-
gracious resemblance to a human foot (*H* 231–32).

"Near as high as the uppermost inhabitant at that time"

Byrd means, of course, the westernmost English inhabitant living
along the line. His position on the evening of 30 October, 1728, would
have been just a little south of the present location of the huge John H.
Kerr Dam, which backs up the Roanoke River for miles to the west.
A later entry, made when the Carolina commissioners and surveyors
withdrew from the expedition on 5 October, comments that they were
fifty miles beyond the last crossing of the Roanoke River, and also
fifty miles "beyond . . . inhabitants" (*SH* 111).

Poisoned fields

Byrd several times distinguishes between fields formerly used
for cultivation by the Indians and what he calls "poisoned fields"—
though no poison appears to have been involved in their creation. His
surmise that the desolated areas may have been caused by fire is probably correct. Forest fires in wilderness areas were sometimes caused by
lightning, but they happened at least as frequently when the campfires

of Native Americans got out of control or when the Indians' method of "fire hunting" resulted in the destruction of large sections of forest. Byrd describes both events in *The History*. He blames many forest fires on the untended campfires of northern Indians who made occasional incursions into the Carolinas to raid the Catawbas and their allies. In a later entry he describes at length the Indians' habit of burning large sections of woods in order to herd deer and other animals toward a point where they might be easily killed. Byrd deplores the practice, but he adds that the "dearth of provisions" later in the journey made the surveying party practice it. (See the entry for 10 November and the comments following it, below.)

"Who commonly prefer the flesh of bears"

Especially in *The Secret History*, Byrd praises the taste and texture of bear meat, and there he reports that the chaplain of the group "loved it so passionately that he would growl like a wildcat over a squirrel" (*SH* 118). Bear meat is much like pork in its texture and taste, and for men on a diet of comparatively dry venison, it must have been a welcome change.

Once the party was beyond the outermost farms and plantations, it depended almost exclusively on wild game for food. Before the Carolina commissioners and surveyors abandoned the survey (on 5 October), the group amounted to thirty-three white men plus the Sapomi Indian Bearskin, who was hired as a professional hunter. Even after the Carolina party left, there were still twenty-six men to feed, and so the larger game animals and birds (principally deer, bear, and turkey) became extremely important.

1 OCTOBER 1728

There was a white frost this morning on the ground, occasioned by a northwest wind, which stood our friend in dispersing all aguish damps and making the air wholesome at the same time that it made it cold. Encouraged, therefore, by the weather, our surveyors got to work early and, by the benefit of clear woods and level ground, drove the line twelve miles and twelve poles.

At a small distance from our camp we crossed Great Creek

and about seven miles farther Nutbush Creek, so called from the many hazel trees growing upon it. By good luck, many branches of these creeks were full of reeds, to the great comfort of our horses. Near five miles from thence we encamped on a branch that runs into Nutbush Creek, where those reeds flourished more than ordinary. The land we marched over was for the most part broken and stony and in some places covered over with thickets almost impenetrable. . . .

One of our Indians killed a large fawn, which was very welcome, though, like Hudibras' horse, it hardly had flesh enough to cover its bones.

In the low grounds the Carolina gentlemen showed us another plant, which they said was used in their country to cure the bite of the rattlesnake. It put forth several leaves in figure like a heart and was clouded so like the common Asarabacca that I conceived it to be of that family (*H* 232–33).

Nutbush Creek

Nutbush Creek is now a large arm of Kerr Reservoir a short distance above the dam. Several state recreation areas and numerous launch ramps make this part of the lake very popular with boaters, campers, and fishermen. The creek reaches twelve miles into North Carolina, almost to the town of Henderson. Its ramps and recreation areas are accessible by state roads leading off of Interstate 85 or North Carolina 39.

What Byrd called nutbushes are actually hazelnut trees or bushes. Hazelnuts (also called filberts) grow on bushes eight to ten feet high. The hazel plant *(Corylus americana)* occurs frequently throughout this section of Virginia and North Carolina.

"A large fawn"

This is the first of twenty-two references to deer in *The History*. The white-tailed deer *(Odocoileus virginianus)* was such a common animal that Byrd wasted almost no time in describing it or speculating about its range, its habits, or its relation to other ungulates. He was obviously more interested in what he saw as slightly more exotic animals such as rattlesnakes, wild turkeys, alligators, wolves, and (most of all) bears. Nevertheless, deer were important for food on the journey, and they were extremely important animals for Native Americans and early European settlers.

Indiscriminate hunting of deer, especially commercial hunting for their hides, resulted in a severe reduction of the animal's numbers in most sections of both Virginia and North Carolina by the early twentieth century. They continued to be plentiful only in the more remote mountain areas and in the swamps to the east. Restoration efforts, begun in both states in the 1940s by livetrapping deer in areas where they were more common then releasing them in suitable habitat, have been enormously successful, however, and white-tailed deer are now common at every point along Byrd's line. As recently as the early 1960s, deer were very rare in most of the border counties. An older resident of Pittsylvania County, Virginia, told me that even finding a deer track in the 1950s and early 1960s was unusual. "You called the neighbors to look at it when you found one," he said. The deer are in his garden almost every night now.

Whereas in 1900 the total population of deer in North Carolina was probably around ten thousand animals, by the late 1990s the number had increased to almost a million. Virginia also supports a population of around a million animals. Today, deer inhabit not only large tracts of forest and swamp but also broken farmland and even vacant land inside cities. The animals are extremely adaptable, and they flourish anywhere there is sufficient cover and food. Deer browse on twigs, honeysuckle, acorns, grapes, greenbrier, the crops in farmers' fields, and suburban flower beds. There are more deer now in almost every county through which Byrd passed than there were when he drew the survey line in 1728.

"Another plant"

Byrd here describes the common wild ginger *(Asarum canadense),* which has heart-shaped leaves and grows in moist, rich grounds in several areas along the line. The root was widely used in folk remedies for indigestion and other ailments. It can also be used as a substitute for ginger in cooking. Wild ginger is scattered throughout the Pied-

mont. Radford et al. list it in the border counties of Warren, Rockingham, and Stokes in North Carolina (*Atlas* 142). I have also found it
growing on my Caswell County farm.

2 OCTOBER 1728

Three miles beyond that we passed another water with difficulty
called Yaptsco or Beaver Creek. Those industrious animals had
dammed up the water so high that we had much ado to get over.
'Tis hardly credible how much work of this kind they will do in
the space of one night. They bite young saplings into proper
lengths with their fore teeth, which are exceeding strong and
sharp, and afterwards drag them to the place where they intend
to stop the water. They know how to join timber and earth together with so much skill that their work is able to resist the
most violent flood that can happen. In this they are qualified to
instruct their betters, it being certain their dams will stand firm
when the strongest that are made by men will be carried down
the stream. We observed very broad, low grounds upon this
creek, with a growth of large trees and all the other signs of fertility, but seemed subject to be everywhere overflowed in a fresh.
The certain way to catch these sagacious animals is this: squeeze
all the juice out of the large pride of the beaver and six drops
out of the small pride. Powder the inward bark of sassafras and
mix it with this juice; then bait therewith a steel trap and they
will eagerly come to it and be taken. . . .

Here we encamped, and by the time the horses were hobbled
our hunters brought us no less than a brace and an half of deer,
which made great plenty and consequently great content in our
quarters. Some of our people had shot a great wildcat, which
was that fatal moment making a comfortable meal upon a fox
squirrel, and an ambitious sportsman of our company claimed
the merit of killing this monster after it was dead. The wildcat is
as big again as any household cat and much the fiercest inhabitant of the woods. Whenever it is disabled, it will tear its own
flesh for madness. Although a panther will run away from a man,
a wildcat will only make a surly retreat, now and then facing

about if he be too closely pursued, and will even pursue in his turn if he observe the least sign of fear or even of caution in those that pretend to follow him. The flesh of this beast, as well as of the panther, is as white as veal and altogether as sweet and delicious (*H* 233–34).

Beaver Creek

There are several creeks and narrow arms of the reservoir now called "Beaver Creek" or "Beaver Dam Creek." The creek Byrd refers to here is probably Island Creek, which forms part of the boundary line between Vance County and Granville County, North Carolina. Beavers are now very active in many of the streams leading into the lake, especially a few miles further west in the areas of Aaron's Creek, Peters Creek, and the Hyco River. (See the discussion in the previous chapter for comments on the comeback of the beaver in both states during the twentieth century.)

The "large pride" and "small pride" of the animals refer to scent-producing glands (which Byrd may have confused with reproductive organs). As Hope Ryden explains, "a beaver's sex organs are concealed in an opening in its abdomen, called the cloaca. This pocket also contains other items of importance to the species. Two pear-shaped glands, which produce a kind of all-purpose substance called castoreum, are located here, as are the animal's anal glands" (35). Both the castor glands and the anal glands are used for scent marking and for posting territory. The "large pride" Byrd mentions is the pair of castor glands; the "small pride" is the pair of anal glands.

Castor from the beaver has always been used as a lure in trapping the animals. The mixture of castor, secretions from the anal glands, and powdered sassafras bark would certainly produce an aromatic blend, whether it would draw beavers or not. Sassafras, a commonly occurring plant throughout the region, has mitten-shaped leaves. Its bark, especially from the root section, smells like licorice.

Wildcat

The wildcat, or bobcat *(Lynx rufus)* is fairly common in the more remote areas along this section of the line, but it is rarely seen, being reclusive and primarily nocturnal. Bobcats are, as Byrd points out, no more than twice as big as a common house cat, but their long legs make them seem much larger. A male might weigh twenty-five pounds or slightly more; the record is a little under forty pounds. The cat's courage and ferocity in a fight gave rise to the expression, "able to lick his weight in wildcats." Bobcats prey principally on squirrels, mice, and other small mammals but will occasionally take turkeys and even small deer.

I have only rarely seen bobcats in the woods, even though I spend many days of the year in areas where they are fairly common and have often encountered their tracks. The first one I saw certainly gave the impression of ferocity in a small package, whether the impression was justified or not. I was bow hunting, waiting in a tree stand near the end of the day, and the cat walked soundlessly into the clearing beneath my stand. I enjoyed the rare spectacle and watched the animal for what seemed like several minutes. When it somehow became aware of my presence, it looked up into the tree, snarled, then walked back into a thicket—altogether too calmly, it seemed to me. On the other hand, one I surprised at close range on the ground several years later beat a hurried and undignified retreat.

I think it is probable that the first cat did not know what I was and therefore appeared unafraid and slow to run away. There is no doubt, though, that a bobcat will attack an animal much larger than itself. A friend told me several years ago that he watched a bobcat make an unsuccessful attempt at taking a medium-sized doe. This was in southern Halifax County, Virginia, very near Byrd's line.

3 OCTOBER 1728

We got to work early this morning and carried the line 8 miles and 160 poles. We forded several runs of excellent water and afterwards traversed a large level of high land, full of lofty walnut, poplar, and white oak trees, which are certain proofs of a fruitful soil. This level was near two miles in length and of an unknown breadth, quite out of danger of being overflowed, which is a misfortune most of the low grounds are liable to in those parts. As we marched along, we saw many buffalo tracks and abundance of their dung very fresh but could not have the pleasure of seeing them. They either smelt us out, having that sense very quick, or else were alarmed at the noise so many people must necessarily make in marching along. At the sight of a man they will snort and grunt, cock up their ridiculous short tails, and tear up the ground with a timorous fury. These wild cattle hardly ever range so far north as forty degrees of latitude, delighting much in canes and reeds which grow generally more southerly (*H* 234–35).

Walnut, poplar, and white oak trees

All three species are indigenous to the area, though large walnut trees *(Juglans nigra)* are no longer easy to find, since the hard, beautifully grained wood is so popular in making fine furniture. The tree commonly called poplar *(Liriodendron tulipifera)* is also known as the tulip tree, the tulip poplar, and the yellow poplar. White oak trees *(Quercus alba)* were often used by early settlers in order to determine the fertility of the soil. The trees prefer rich, well-drained soil that makes good farming land.

Buffalo

Byrd mentions buffalo several times in both manuscripts, and he was obviously fascinated by the big animals. They must have been very easy to hunt, however, as they were almost completely eliminated from areas near white settlements within a few decades of his writing. According to Edward Nickens, the last buffalo *(Bison bison)* in North Carolina was killed near Asheville in 1799 (15).

4 OCTOBER 1728

We hurried away the surveyors about nine this morning, who extended the line 7 miles and 160 poles, notwithstanding the ground was exceedingly uneven. At the distance of five miles we forded a stream to which we gave the name of Bluewing Creek because of the great number of those fowls that then frequented it. About two and a half miles beyond that, we came upon Sugartree Creek, so called from the many trees of that kind that grow

upon it. By tapping this tree in the first warm weather in Febru-
ary, one may get from twenty to forty gallons of liquor, very
sweet to the taste and agreeable to the stomach. This may be
boiled into molasses first and afterwards into very good sugar,
allowing about ten gallons of liquor to make a pound. There is
no doubt, too, that a very fine spirit may be distilled from the
molasses, at least as good as rum. The sugar tree delights only in
rich ground, where it grows very tall, and by the softness and
sponginess of the wood should be a quick grower. Near this
creek we discovered likewise several spice trees, the leaves of
which are fragrant and the berries they bear are black when dry
and of a hot taste, not much unlike pepper. . . .

One of our men spied three buffaloes, but his piece being
loaded only with goose shot, he was able to make no effectual
impression on their thick hides; however, this disappointment
was made up by a brace of bucks and as many wild turkeys killed
by the rest of the company. Thus Providence was very bountiful
to our endeavors, never disappointing those that faithfully rely
upon it and pray heartily for their daily bread (*H* 235–36).

Bluewing Creek

This creek is located in the southeastern section of present-day
Halifax County, Virginia. It crosses the line just east of Mayo Reservoir, on the Halifax, Virginia/Person County, North Carolina, line.
The "great numbers of those fowls" frequenting it were blue-winged
teal *(Anas discors)*, a small, colorful duck that migrates through this area
much earlier than most of the larger ducks, usually arriving in late
September or early October—about the time Byrd and his men were
passing through the area.

Sugar tree

Byrd refers to the sugar maple *(Acer saccharum)* that occurs commonly throughout this area. A related species, the southern sugar
maple *(A. barbatum)*, is found chiefly in the coastal plain. There are several creeks along this latitude still called Sugartree Creek.

Spice trees

The "tree" described here is a large, bushy shrub commonly called the spice bush *(Lindera benzoin)*. It is a member of the laurel family, bearing yellow flowers in the spring and small red fruit in the fall. Like another member of the laurel family, sassafras, this plant has a spicy odor in all its parts—buds, bark, and berries. Native Americans and early settlers made varied use of the spice bush. Oil from the berries, berry tea, and teas made from the bark and twigs were thought to be remedies for ailments ranging from coughs and colds to rheumatism and typhoid fever. Furthermore, the berries were sometimes used as a substitute for allspice (Foster and Duke 252).

"His piece being loaded only with goose shot"

Most firearms in the eighteenth century had smooth (as opposed to rifled) bores. Typically, a firearm carried by a Virginian or North Carolinian in the early 1700s would have been a single-barreled flintlock of large caliber, with a bore diameter of between .60 and .75 inches. Later, when the frontier was being pushed ever farther westward, smaller calibers, usually ranging from about .50 down to about .36, came into common use, since the weapon's owner would need a smaller total volume of lead and powder in order to provide food and protection. This was particularly the case after the use of rifled barrels, affording much greater accuracy, became common.

The advantages of the large-caliber smoothbores lay in the speed with which they could be reloaded in an emergency and in their suitability for handling either shot or single balls. If the shooter anticipated small game or birds, he would be likely to use a measure of shot; if he anticipated shooting large game, he would certainly use a full-caliber ball. "Goose shot" would be fairly coarse shot (probably corresponding to about modern size #2 lead shot, though nothing was standardized in the 1720s), and it would be suitable for collecting a wide variety of animals and birds, up to and including the wild turkeys that are mentioned so often in this section. It would, as Byrd notes, be of no use whatsoever against a buffalo.

5 OCTOBER 1728

This day we met with such uneven grounds and thick underwoods that with all our industry we were able to advance the
line but 4 miles and 312 poles. In this small distance it intersected a large stream four times, which our Indian at first mis-
took for the south branch of Roanoke River; but, discovering
his error soon after, he assured us 'twas a river called Hycootomony, or Turkey Buzzard River, from the great number of those
unsavory birds that roost on the tall trees growing near its banks.

Early in the afternoon, to our very great surprise, the commissioners of Carolina acquainted us with their resolution to return
home (*H* 236).

Hycootomony, or Turkey Buzzard River

This is another name for the Hyco River, and Byrd shortens the
name to Hyco for the rest of his narrative (Wright 105). The Hyco
River now flows out of Hyco Reservoir, in Person County, North Carolina, and runs northeastward into Virginia. A few miles later, it flows
into a part of the Dan River now flooded by Kerr Reservoir.

"Their resolution to return home"

The Carolina commissioners reasoned that since the line had run
some 170 miles from Currituck Inlet, the two parties had agreed on
the location of Weyanoke Creek, and the last white settler was now
fifty miles behind the present position, they had done all that was required. Byrd disagreed, and although he glosses over the disagree-
ment in *The History*, only adding a few comments to his narration from
time to time regarding the unpleasant nature of the Carolina commissioners, in *The Secret History* he devotes several pages to the argument.
He also includes a copy of a letter signed by four of the Carolina party
and a rejoinder to it that he wrote and that he and William Dandridge
both signed.

7 OCTOBER 1728

In this small distance we crossed the Hyco the fifth time and
quartered near Buffalo Creek, so named from the frequent

tokens we discovered of that American behemoth. Here the
bushes were so intolerably thick that we were obliged to cover
the bread bags with our deerskins, otherwise the joke of one of
the Indians must have happened to us in good earnest: that in a
few days we must cut up our house to make bags for the bread
and so be forced to expose our backs in compliment to our
bellies. We computed we had then biscuit enough left to last us,
with good management, seven weeks longer; and this being our
chief dependence, it imported us to be very careful both in the
carriage and the distribution of it. . . .

Our men killed a very fat buck and several turkeys. These two
kinds of meat boiled together, with the addition of a little rice
or French barley, made excellent soup, and, what happens rarely
in other good things, it never cloyed, no more than an engaging
wife would do, by being a constant dish. . . .

We observed abundance of coltsfoot and maidenhair in many
places and nowhere a larger quantity than here. They are both
excellent pectoral plants and seem to have greater virtues much
in this part of the world than in more northern climates; and I
believe it may pass for a rule in botanics that where any vegetable
is planted by the hand of Nature it has more virtue than in places
whereto it is transplanted by the curiosity of man (*H* 238–39).

Buffalo Creek

Wright suggests that Buffalo Mineral Springs, in Halifax County,
Virginia, "is believed to have received its name from Byrd's description
of the buffalo he saw nearby" (113). Byrd's position on 7 October was
south of present-day South Boston, Virginia, about two miles west of
U.S. 501.

Coltsfoot and maidenhair

Byrd was ever on the lookout for medicinal plants, and both of
these are commonly used for chest and bronchial ailments. Coltsfoot
(Tussilago farfara) has been used since ancient times to treat bronchial
disorders, usually by boiling down the leaves. Pliny (whom Byrd had
certainly read) recommended smoking the dried leaves for relief of

coughs and congestion. The only problem is that coltsfoot is not a native plant; it was introduced from Europe during colonial times. Byrd must surely have been looking at some other plant that he confused with the familiar coltsfoot.

Maidenhair fern *(Adiantum pedantum)* grows all along both sides of the line from the lower Piedmont into the mountains. A European relative of *A. pedantum,* also called maidenhair fern *(A. capillus veneris),* has, like the coltsfoot, a long history of use in treating lung problems. The latter plant has often been grown as an ornamental in gardens as well as for its medicinal qualities. This probably explains Byrd's comment about the wild plant's having "more virtue than in places whereto it has been transplanted by the curiosity of man."

8 OCTOBER 1728

> We quartered near a spring of very fine water, as soft as oil and as cold as ice, to make us amends for the want of wine. And our Indian knocked us down a very fat doe, just time enough to hinder us from going supperless to bed. . . .
>
> We were entertained this night with the yell of a whole family of wolves, in which we could distinguish the treble, tenor, and bass very clearly. These beasts of prey kept pretty much upon our track, being tempted by the garbage of the creatures we killed every day, for which we were serenaded with their shrill pipes almost every night. This beast is not so untamable as the panther, but the Indians know how to gentle their whelps and use them about their cabins instead of dogs (*H* 239–40).

Wolves

Again, Byrd refers to the red wolves once common throughout the southeast. (See the discussion in chapter 1.) The observation about Indians taming whelps and using them for dogs is possibly correct, but it is more likely that Native Americans, having long since domesticated the dog, would have had little use for wolf pups, which usually grow up to be intractable. Wolves can mate with dogs and produce fertile offspring, however, and it may be that Byrd saw some of these wolf/dog crosses in Indian villages.

9 OCTOBER 1728

The thickets were hereabouts so impenetrable that we were obliged, at first setting-off this morning, to order four pioneers to clear the way before the surveyors. But after about two miles of these rough woods, we had the pleasure to meet with open grounds, and not very uneven, by the help of which we were enabled to push the line about six miles. The baggage that lay short of our camp last night came up about noon, and the men made heavy complaints that they had been half-starved, like Tantalus in the midst of plenty, for the reason above-mentioned.

The soil we passed over this day was generally good, being clothed with large trees of poplar, hickory, and oak. But another certain token of its fertility was that wild angelica grew plentifully upon it. The root of this plant, being very warm and aromatic, is coveted by woodsmen extremely as a dram, that is, when rum, that cordial for all distresses, is wanting.

A great flock of cranes flew over our quarters, that were exceeding clamorous in their flight. They seem to steer their course toward the south (being birds of passage) in quest of warmer weather. They only took this country in their way, being as rarely met with in this part of the world as a highwayman or a beggar. These birds travel generally in flocks, and when they roost they place sentinels upon some of the highest trees, which constantly stand upon one leg to keep themselves waking. . . .

Our Indian killed nothing all day but a mountain partridge, which a little resembled the common partridge in the plumage but was near as large as a dunghill hen. These are very frequent toward the mountains, though we had the fortune to meet with very few (*H* 240–41).

Wild angelica

It is difficult to imagine exactly what Byrd found here, or what use he thought it really had. There are several ferns called angelica, and some of them are highly poisonous. The woody plant called the Hercules club or the devil's walking stick is also known as the angelica tree. It is sometimes used in folk medicine, but not in the way Byrd suggests. The berries are poisonous, though they were sometimes used for treating toothaches. The roots were made into a poultice for treating skin eruptions and boils (Foster and Duke 238). There is a plant called wild angelica *(Angelica atropurpurea)* traditionally used to treat stomachaches and indigestion, but it is not generally found any farther south than Delaware and West Virginia. Radford et al. describe it as "rare" in the area and list only Haywood County, in the high mountains of North Carolina, as a locale where it may be found *(Manual* 786). It is unlikely that Byrd discovered it east of the Dan River. *A. atropurpurea* somewhat resembles several other plants that do occur in the area, including the water hemlock *(Cicuta maculata),* which is extremely poisonous.

Cranes

The word *crane* was (and sometimes still is) used loosely to describe any number of large, long-necked wading birds, especially the great blue heron. However, Byrd's details make it improbable that he is describing herons here. More likely, he saw a migrating flock of sandhill cranes *(Grus canadensis).* Sandhill cranes are very large (up to four feet high) and were common in the Midwest during the early eighteenth century. They wintered in the Deep South and perhaps as far north as southern North Carolina. Most of the cranes now breeding in the Midwest and Northwest winter in Florida and extreme southern Georgia. It should be noted that Byrd seems a little surprised to see them so far north. He would not have been surprised at seeing the great blue heron. Also, his description of the loud cries of the birds in flight fits the sandhill crane perfectly. Some of the great birds still pass through Virginia and North Carolina on their way to wintering grounds in Florida. Most of the migration is to the west of Byrd's position here, however.

Mountain Partridge

Byrd describes a grouse *(Bonasa umbellus),* which does indeed look much like a very large quail. (Quail are sometimes called partridges even today in many parts of the South.) Grouse are found in the mountains of both Virginia and North Carolina but almost never as far into the Piedmont as Byrd's location on the ninth of October. I was unable to determine whether the range of the bird commonly extended farther eastward during the colonial period. Probably not, as even William Byrd seems surprised by its appearance.

10 OCTOBER 1728

A small distance from our camp we crossed a pleasant stream of water called Cockade Creek, and something more than a mile from thence our line intersected the Dan. It was about two hundred yards wide where we forded it, and when we came over to the west side we found the banks lined with a forest of tall canes that grew more than a furlong in depth. So that it cost us abundance of time and labor to cut a passage through them wide enough for our baggage.

In the meantime, we had leisure to take a full view of this charming river. The stream, which was perfectly clear, ran down about two knots, or two miles, an hour when the water was at the lowest. The bottom was covered with a coarse gravel, spangled very thick with a shining substance that almost dazzled the eye, and the sand upon either shore sparkled with the same splendid particles. At first sight, the sunbeams, giving a yellow cast to these spangles, made us fancy them to be gold dust and consequently that all our fortunes were made. . . .

We marched about two miles and a half beyond this river as far as Cane Creek, so called from a prodigious quantity of tall canes that fringed the banks of it. On the west side of this creek we marked out our quarters and were glad to find our horses fond of the canes, though they scoured them smartly at first and discolored their dung. This common vegetable grows commonly from thirteen to sixteen feet high, and some of them as thick as a man's wrist (*H* 242–43).

Cockade Creek

Byrd explains in *The Secret History* that the creek was so named "from our beginning there to wear the turkey beard in our hats by way of cockade" (*SH* 139). Cockade Creek is now called Country Line Creek, and it winds through much of Caswell County, North Carolina, emptying into the Dan River a mile from my house. The wild turkeys Byrd describes as so common in the woods near this creek, having almost disappeared from the entire area in the early twentieth century, are now back in significant numbers, and I see them frequently. (See also the discussion of the return of wild-turkey population to the area in the comment for Byrd's entry of 23 September, above.)

Dan

The Dan River now runs principally through farmland in this area. Farmland does not hold soil as well as virgin forest does, and consequently the river is never clear. It is also deeper and more narrow at this point than in Byrd's description of it, a result of modern farmers' and landowners' need to keep the Dan in a more-or-less predictable channel, so that the banks on either side can be used for agriculture.

Just upstream from the point where Byrd first crossed the Dan, a few hundred yards above the North Carolina 62 bridge into Milton, one can find the remains of an Indian fish trap. The trap was made of stones placed almost all the way across the river to form a V shape, with the point of the V downstream. Fish moving downstream would be directed into wicker baskets placed at the end of the trap. Rountree describes identical traps along in the Potomac, the Rappahannock, and the James Rivers. Many of the stones making up the trap are still visible during times of very low water.

Cane Creek

Cane Creek flows into the Dan a few hundred yards south of the line. There are still thickets of cane growing along the banks of the Dan near Cane Creek and in other places, though they are nowhere a furlong deep. The cane he refers to is the common cane, *Arundinaria gigantea,* often called "reed cane" or (incorrectly) "bamboo cane" locally. Children often make fishing poles out of the slender canes. *Arundinaria* grows all over North Carolina and Virginia, especially in low, moist ground.

3 ❋ "THE LAND OF FAT BEAR"

The Dan River to the Mountains

BYRD'S LINE crossed the winding valley of the Dan River five times in the next twenty-two miles of surveying. Then, just a few miles west and south of the present-day city of Danville, Virginia, the Dan dropped "more southerly with a very flush and plentiful stream, the description whereof must be left to future discoveries" (*H* 252). The surveyors continued westward, crossing and naming Cascade Creek, Matrimony Creek, the Irvin River, and the Mayo River. (The Irvin has since been renamed the Smith River.) The men worked through 26 October, extending the line to a point six miles south of what is now Stuart, Virginia. The length of the line, Byrd observes in *The History,* was 240 miles and 230 poles (about 240.7 miles), from its origin at Currituck Inlet to its termination. (Byrd was not entirely consistent in his several accounts of the distance. See the discussion on his entry of 26 October, below.)

In many ways this is the most enthusiastic section of both accounts. Byrd is in high spirits. The men are, for most of the journey, eating well, feasting on venison, wild turkey, and bear meat, drinking clear water from the rivers and streams they come to, and obviously enjoying their rare fortune in seeing territory few other white men have ever seen. Byrd comments at length on their diet and their dispositions, and he makes lengthy notes on what he learns from the hunter, Bearskin, about Saponi religious beliefs.

Among the wildlife he describes in this section are geese, panthers, passenger pigeons, raccoons, opossums, elk, four kinds of squirrels, and the ever-present bears. He writes several pages about the Indians' habit of scalping enemies and their methods of torturing prisoners. He names bodies of water whimsically (Matrimony Creek was "called so by an unfortunate married man because it was extremely noisy and impetuous") or by giving creeks and rivers the names of members of the surveying party.

Byrd mentions seeing mountains for the first time as early as the eleventh of October, when he is still to the east of present-day Danville. "Astrolabe [William Mayo, one of the surveyors] discovered them very plain to the northwest of our course, though at a great distance" (*SH* 117). The only mountains visible from this location, and in that direction, would have been White Oak Mountain, which rises to a height of only about a thousand feet, and beyond that Turkeycock Mountain, a few hundred feet higher. Within three more days, however, the party was beyond the Dan, and by the afternoon of the fourteenth they came to a high point of ground "that commanded a full prospect of the mountains and an extensive view of the flat country."

From this point westward the land began getting steeper, and both the horses and the men would soon have a more difficult time traveling. Byrd describes the vistas with enthusiasm, mentioning "a beautiful range of hills, as level as a table walk, that overlooks the valley through which Crooked Creek conveys its spiral stream" (*H* 265). A mountain to the south of the line "so vastly high it seemed to hide its head in the clouds" was given the romantic name "Despairing Lover's Leap." Another mountain looked like "a vast stack of chimneys." Climbing a mountain at the end of their journey and looking westward, the men were able to see the Blue Ridge range very plainly only thirty miles away. Only the lack of provisions, the necessity of returning before winter set in, and the poor condition of the horses prevented further westward exploration of "that place, which the hand of Nature made so remarkable" (*H* 268).

Visitors to this section of the dividing line today can glimpse the same mountains that Byrd's party saw by traveling west on U.S. 58 from Danville, Virginia. Just beyond the city limits, one can see White Oak Mountain to the north of town and Turkeycock Mountain to the northwest. Taking the Berry Hill Road to the southwest, the visitor will cross over into North Carolina near Byrd's last crossing of the Dan, then over Cascade Creek, on North Carolina 770, a half mile from where Byrd crossed it in 1728. (It is still filled with the black slate rock he described.) The highway will lead to the little town of Eden, built on land once owned by Byrd—land that he secured for himself shortly after his return from the surveying expedition. North Carolina 87 out of Eden will cross back into Virginia near the Smith River (which Byrd called the Irvin) and a few miles later will afford a clear view of Chestnut Knob, the mountain Byrd named "the Wart."

Virginia 87 will connect with U.S. 220, then with U.S. 58 just beyond Chestnut Knob, the rest of the way toward Stuart presenting a constant panorama of mountains to the north and west. To the south, as Byrd noted, individual peaks arise, whereas to the north the Blue Ridge seems to form a wall of mountains.

Virginia 8 leads due south out of Stuart and, just before it crosses the state line into North Carolina, provides a clear view of the mountain Byrd named "Despairing Lover's Leap," now called Moore's Knob, in Stokes County. Byrd was very near Peters Creek, about two miles west of where Virginia 8 intersects the line. At this point they marked the end of the line: "The last tree we marked was a red oak growing on the bank of the river; and to make the place more remarkable, we blazed all the trees around it" (*H* 268).

It would still be almost a month before the survey party was able to get home, traveling back along the same route through the Dan River valley and finally reaching the edges of civilization again near the Nottoway River. During those weeks, Byrd would make more observations about the plants and animals he encountered. But it is obvious that he felt a sense of elation at having run the line as far as he did, and his enthusiasm in later sections is never as great as it is here. The journey home would be full of anticipation of the joy of seeing loved ones again, but it would also be a little sad. The great adventure was almost over.

11 OCTOBER 1728

At the distance of four miles and sixty poles from the place
where we encamped, we came upon the river Dan a second time,

though it was not so wide in this place as where we crossed it first, being not above 150 yards over. The west shore continued to be covered with the canes above mentioned but not to so great a breadth as before, and 'tis remarkable that these canes are much more frequent on the west side of the river than on the east, where they grow generally very scattering. It was still a beautiful stream, rolling down its limpid and murmuring waters among the rocks, which lay scattered here and there to make up the variety of the prospect.

It was about two miles from this river to the end of our day's work, which led us mostly over broken grounds and troublesome underwoods. Hereabout, from one of the highest hills we made the first discovery of the mountains on the northwest of our course. They seemed to lie off at a vast distance and looked like ranges of blue clouds rising one above another.

We encamped about two miles beyond the river, where we made good cheer upon a very fat buck that luckily fell in our way. The Indian likewise shot a wild turkey but confessed he would not bring it us lest we should continue to provoke the guardian of the forest by cooking the beasts of the field and the birds of the air together in one vessel. This instance of Indian superstition, I confess, is countenanced by the Levitical law, which forbade the mixing things of a different nature together in the same field or in the same garment, and why not, then, in the same kettle? But, after all, if the jumbling of two sorts of flesh together be a sin, how intolerable an offense it must be to make a Spanish olla, that is, a hotchpotch of every kind of thing that is eatable? And the good people of England would have a good deal to answer for for beating up so many different ingredients into a pudding (H 244).

"Not above 150 yards over"

The Dan is no more than eighty yards wide below Danville now, where Byrd crossed. There are three dams in Danville which help govern the flow of water and keep the river more or less channeled, except during periods after unusually heavy rains. It looks like a typical Piedmont stream as it flows through the farming country east and south of the city. The banks of the river are lined with tall trees, and the understory is thick with vines and, in places, the canes Byrd mentions. The trees and thick undergrowth end a few dozen yards from the river's edge in most places, giving way to pastures and fields.

The Dan could by no means be called "limpid" now, and the only places its water murmurs over rocks are near the boulders that rise up now and then from the water. The average depth in this section is around three to four feet. From Byrd's description, it must have been somewhat shallower and considerably wider in the early eighteenth century. The site of Byrd's second crossing of the river is a mile south of the Danville airport.

"First discovery of the mountains"

The only mountains usually visible to the northwest of the city are the broken string of hills making up White Oak Mountain, which rises to a height of just under 1,000 feet. Beyond White Oak Mountain, six or seven miles to the northwest, lies Turkeycock Mountain, nearly twice that high. Much farther to the north is Smith Mountain, also around 1,800 feet high. In all probability Byrd was seeing the tops of White Oak Mountain and perhaps, beyond that, Turkeycock Mountain. The observer's own elevation on any of the more prominent hills near the Dan River could have been no more than about 600 feet. Byrd was standing on one of the hills in what is now called the "Mountain Hill" community, just east and south of Danville.

After years of living in tidewater Virginia, Byrd may indeed have regarded White Oak and Turkeycock as looking like "ranges of blue clouds rising one above the other." Within days, though, he would see and record much more impressive peaks.

White Oak Mountain Wildlife Management Area, located about fifteen miles north of the city, includes 2,700 acres of land, including some of the high ground Byrd was able to see. Another management area of about the same size is located on Turkeycock Mountain. Both areas sustain substantial populations of deer, turkey, and small game, though the bears, wolves, panthers, and buffalo Byrd described in the area have long since disappeared.

"Beasts of the field and birds of the air"

The Indian hunter Bearskin had earlier told the party that it was not proper to cook deer and turkeys together, giving Byrd an opportunity here to draw a parallel between Biblical tradition and the Native American prohibition, as he does in his treatise on comparative religion two days later, on 13 October. In *The Secret History,* however, he is less patient, dismissing the Indian's hesitation to make venison and turkey stew as "ridiculous superstition."

12 OCTOBER 1728

We were so cruelly entangled with bushes and grapevines all day that we could advance the line no farther than five miles and twenty-eight poles. The vines grew very thick in these woods, twining lovingly round the trees almost everywhere, especially to the saplings. This makes it evident how natural both the soil and climate of this country are to vines, though I believe most to our own vines. The grapes we commonly met with were black, though there be two or three kinds of white grape that grow wild. The black are very sweet but small, because the strength of the vine spends itself in wood, though without question a proper culture would make the same grapes both larger and sweeter. But, with all these disadvantages, I have drunk tolerable good wine pressed from them, though made without skill. There is then good reason to believe it might admit of great improvement if rightly managed.

Our Indian killed a bear, two years old, that was feasting on these grapes. He was very fat, as they generally are in that season of the year. In the fall the flesh of this animal has a high relish different from that of other creatures, though inclining nearest to that of pork, or rather of wild boar. A true woodsman prefers this sort of meat to that of the fattest venison, not only for the haut gout, but also because the fat of it is well tasted and never rises in the stomach. Another proof of the goodness of this

meat is that it is less apt to corrupt than any other we are acquainted with.

As agreeable as such rich diet was to the men, yet we who
were not accustomed to it tasted it at first with some sort of
squeamishness, that animal being of the dog kind, though a little
use soon reconciled us to this American version. And that its
being of the dog kind might give us the less disgust, we had the
example of that ancient and polite people, the Chinese, who
reckon the dog's flesh too good for any under the quality of a
mandarin. . . .

They are naturally not carnivorous, unless hunger constrain
them to it after the mast is all gone and the product of the
woods quite exhausted. . . . Their errand then is to surprise a
poor hog at a pinch to keep them from starving. . . .

But bears soon grow weary of this unnatural diet, and about
January, when there is nothing to be gotten in the woods, they
retire into some cave or hollow tree, where they sleep away two
or three months very comfortably. But then they quit their holes
in March, when the fish begin to fill up the rivers, on which
they are forced to keep Lent till some fruit or berry comes in
season. But bears are fondest of chestnuts, which grow plentifully toward the mountains, upon very large trees, where the soil
happens to be rich. We were curious to know how it happened
that many of the outward branches of those trees came to be
broke off in that solitary place and were informed that the bears
are so discreet as not to trust their unwieldy bodies on the
smaller limbs of the tree that would not bear their weight, but
after venturing as far as is safe, which they can judge to an inch,
they bite off the end of the branch, which falling down, they are
content to finish their repast upon the ground. In the same cau-
tious manner they secure the acorns that grow on the weaker
limbs of the oak. And it must be allowed that in these instances
a bear carries instinct a great way and acts more reasonably than
many of his betters, who indiscreetly venture upon frail projects
that won't bear them (*H* 244–46).

"Grapes we commonly met with were black"

The muscadine, or wild scuppernong grape *(Vitis rotundifolia),* ripens in late September and early October in this area—precisely when Byrd was passing through. It is a black or nearly black grape with a thick skin, and it is very sweet—the only really sweet wild grape encountered here. The grapes grow singly or in small bunches of two or three on thick, woody vines that reach into the tallest trees. Where the trees are lower, the vines may form dense, tangled thickets. In more open forest areas, large vines twine through the upper story of oak and hickory trees. The lower trunks of muscadine vines can be nearly as thick as a man's wrist. In the early fall the sweet, musky smell of the grapes can be detected several yards from the trees on which the vines grow. The ground underneath the vines is often littered with fallen grapes, and many animals, including deer, bear, and squirrels, feed on them. Byrd notes that one of the bears killed by the party was taken as it was feeding on these wild grapes.

Wright points out that the English colonists "made continuing efforts to develop a wine industry. The first explorers of the American continent were impressed by the abundance of grapes, and from the time of Raleigh's expeditions until the end of the colonial period efforts were made to plant vineyards and produce wine. Byrd's brother-in-law, Robert Beverly, attempted to establish a vineyard, as did other Virginians, including Byrd himself" (244n).

Thomas Harriot, in the 1590 edition of *A Briefe and True Report of the New Found Land of Virginia,* waxed enthusiastic about the possibility of vineyards in the New World. Comparing the muscadine to smaller wild grapes, he said, "There are two kinds of grapes that the soil doth yeeld naturally: the one is small and sowre of the ordinaire bigness as ours in England: the other farre greater and of himself lushious sweet. When they are planted and husbanded as they ought, a principall commoditie of wines by them may be raised" (9).

"Our Indian killed a bear"

Anyone reading Byrd's report today must wonder at the prodigious quantity of large animals he describes, especially bears. He was, of course, traveling through territory that was largely unexplored, and the animals had had little exposure to human beings.

Bears are only occasionally found in this section of the Dan River valley now. When they do appear, they are almost always emigrants from the swamp forests of eastern North Carolina or, less frequently, from more mountainous areas of Virginia. I have seen only one in the area in recent years (a victim of truck traffic along U.S. 58), but I have seen tracks and droppings occasionally, and reports of bear sightings occur from time to time. One of my neighbors saw a bear eating her dog's food a few years ago. She called the wildlife agency, and the bear was subsequently trapped and relocated to a region with fewer civilized temptations.

Due to intensive management efforts and the setting aside of large wilderness tracts of swamp as bear sanctuaries, the population of bears in eastern North Carolina approximately doubled during the 1970s and nearly doubled again by the middle 1990s, with the result that some black bears, forced to seek new territory, traveled up the great river corridors, including the Roanoke/Dan, into areas from which they had been absent for a century.

In Virginia and North Carolina black bears inhabit the mountains and the lowland swamps, and in some parts of their range they are fairly numerous. Virginia now has a total population of about 3,500–5,000 of the animals, and North Carolina, with as many as 7,500–10,000, has the largest number of any of the southeastern states. The densest population of bears is in southeastern Virginia and northeastern North Carolina, from the Great Dismal Swamp southward through the Albemarle Peninsula and down through Craven and Carteret Counties.

"Bears are fondest of chestnuts"

Bears were indeed fond of chestnuts in previous periods, but many large stands of chestnut trees *(Castanea dentata)* were cut by logging operations in the early twentieth century, and the imported chestnut blight had destroyed almost all the rest of the mature trees by the early 1930s. The roots of blighted trees continue to send up shoots, but they never again become trees capable of producing chestnuts—much less supporting the weight of bears.

Before the beginning of the chestnut blight around 1904, the huge trees were among the most common large hardwoods in eastern forests. They were also among the most important, both for their wood and for their fruit, upon which (as Byrd points out) many animals, including bears, fed.

One of the most encouraging notes for dendrologists recently concerns the efforts of the American Chestnut Foundation to restore the great trees to eastern and southeastern forests. In 2000 and 2001 researchers began planting trees that were crosses of Chinese and American chestnuts in suitable habitat. Among the sites selected were mountainous areas near Asheville, North Carolina, and along the Tennessee border. The Chinese variety is blight resistant, and researchers have "backcrossed" the Chinese and American varieties, producing a tree that has the characteristics of an American chestnut. So far, the trees have proved blight resistant. Paul Sisco, a geneticist for the Foundation, says that the most recently planted seeds are 84 percent American and that the group hopes to be working with trees that are 94 percent American within five years ("Chestnut Trees" 33). The American Chestnut Foundation's website can be accessed at www.acf.org.

Fortunately, the animals that depended on the great chestnut trees and their large, sweet nuts were adaptable. Bears feed on all hard mast, including beechnuts and several different kinds of acorns, and they also eat berries, grapes, wild plums, and other soft mast; near settled areas they often raid cornfields and other crops. They tend to be omnivorous, and various small mammals, as well as reptiles and amphibians, can be included in their diets. I have seen the remains of a small deer which had been eaten by a bear, but I could not tell whether the bear had caught and killed the deer or the deer had been wounded or killed previously. Biologists in the Great Smoky Mountains National Park point out that bears are opportunists and will kill and eat young deer when they can. As Byrd notes, a few bears occasionally cause problems on farms by killing hogs, but the vast majority of their intake is vegetable rather than animal matter.

Bears are very curious, and their tastes seem to be guided in part by curiosity and opportunism. They have several times broken into an isolated hunting and fishing camp of mine in Tyrrell County, North Carolina. Once inside the cabin, they have sampled duck decoys, metal tool-storage chests, mattresses, articles of clothing, and other inedible items, leaving tooth marks and/or shredding the items in a frustrated attempt to find something worth their efforts. On none of the occasions when they entered the cabin were there any foodstuffs left behind to attract them; they were apparently motivated entirely by curiosity and the hope that there *might* be something left inside. Like Byrd, I find bears fascinating creatures, and I do not begrudge the occasional mess and the loss of personal items. Such losses are a small price to pay to have bears as neighbors.

13 OCTOBER 1728

In the afternoon our hunters went forth and returned triumphantly with three brace of wild turkeys. They told us they could see the mountains distinctly from every eminence, though the atmosphere was so thick with smoke that they appeared at a greater distance than they really were.

In the evening we examined our friend Bearskin concerning the religion of his country, and he explained it to us without any of that reserve to which his nation is subject. He told us he believed there was one supreme god, who had subaltern deities under him. And that this master god made the world a long time ago. That he told the sun, the moon, and stars their business in the beginning, which they, with good looking-after, have faithfully performed ever since. . . .

He believed that after death both good and bad people are conducted by a strong guard into a great road, in which departed souls travel together for some time till at a certain distance this road forks into two paths, the one extremely level and the other stony and mountainous. Here the good are parted from the bad by a flash of lightning, the first being hurried away to the right, the other to the left. The right-hand road leads to a charming, warm country, where the spring is everlasting and every

month is May; and as the year is always in its youth, so are the
people, and particularly the women are bright as stars and never
scold. That in this happy climate there are deer, turkeys, elks,
and buffaloes innumerable, perpetually fat and gentle, while the
trees are loaded with delicious fruit quite throughout the four
seasons. . . . The left-hand path is very rugged and uneven, leading to a dark and barren country where it is always winter. The
ground is the whole year round covered with snow, and nothing
is to be seen upon the trees but icicles. All the people are hungry
yet have not a morsel of anything to eat except a bitter kind of
potato, that gives them the dry gripes and fills their whole body
with loathsome divers ulcers that stink and are insupportably
painful. Here all the women are old and ugly, having claws like a
panther with which they fly upon the men that slight their passion. For it seems these haggard old furies are intolerably fond
and expect a vast deal of cherishing. They talk much and exceedingly shrill, giving exquisite pain to the drum of the ear,
which in that place of the torment is so tender that every sharp
note wounds it to the quick. At the end of this path sits a dreadful old woman on a monstrous toadstool, whose head is covered
with rattlesnakes instead of tresses, with glaring white eyes that
strike a terror unspeakable into all that behold her. This hag
pronounces sentence of woe upon all the miserable wretches that
hold up their hands at her tibunal. After this they are delivered
over to huge turkey buzzards, like harpies, that fly away with
them to the place above-mentioned. Here, after they have been
tormented a certain number of years according to their several
degrees of guilt, they are again driven back into this world to
try if they will mend their manners and merit a place the next
time in the regions of bliss (*H* 246–48).

"The atmosphere was so thick with smoke"

What seems a casual observation is really Byrd's voicing evidence
of a major concern. He points out elsewhere that fires were often
set by raiding parties of northern Indians who traveled through the
area on their way to make war with the Catawbas and other southern

tribes. He was understandably anxious to avoid a confrontation with one of these raiding parties. (See his entry and the comments for 20 October, below.) The mountains visible to the party on 13 October would have been those just to the south and west of present-day Martinsville, Virginia.

"Concerning the religion of his country"

Byrd's lively, eighteenth-century gentleman's curiosity about anything novel (including religious beliefs) is nowhere better expressed than in his discussion of Bearskin's religion. Like the good rationalist he was, he tries to understand everything he sees and hears in relation to what he already knows. Thus he draws parallels between Saponi traditional beliefs and those of Christianity and Islam, concluding that, though the Indian tradition is all that "could be expected from a mere state of nature" (that is, as opposed to divine revelation), it "contained, however, the three great articles of natural religion: the belief of a god, the moral distinction between good and evil, and the expectations of rewards and punishments in another world" (*H* 248). In fact Byrd's approach to understanding Bearskin's religion is not very different from his approach to understanding the animals and plants he encounters on his journey.

Wright points out that William Strachey's account of the Powhatan Indian beliefs in an afterlife "has some points of resemblance with Bearskin's religion" (*SH* 118, n. 82). One might also observe that Byrd's rendering of the Saponi afterlife, with its forking road, sounds strikingly like the account in Vergil's *Aeneid,* Book Six. The Sibyl tells Aeneas a remarkably similar tale: "This is the place where the road goes in two different directions. The path to the right skirts the dwelling place of mighty Dis and points the way to Elysium. The other to the left inflicts punishment on the wicked and sends them to godless Tartarus." With his constant love of categorizing and comparing information, Byrd would naturally have been attracted to Bearskin's account. Whether he modified that account to fit a construction with which he was familiar is impossible to say.

In fact Byrd's rendering sounds a great deal more like Vergil than like the record of many other early writers' accounts of Virginia Indians' belief in the afterlife, including those of John Smith. Rountree says that the "Powhatans did not believe in separate afterlives for the good and the wicked, and they were confused by 'leading' English questions about such things" (139). Thomas Harriot, on the other hand, in his 1590 *Brief and True Preport* of the coastal Carolina Algonquins, said that the Indians "beleeve also in the immortalitie of the soule, that after this life as soon as the soule is departed from the body, according the workes it hath done, it is either carried to heaven the habitacle of the gods, there to enjoy perpetual blisse and happinesse, or els to a great pitte or hole, which they think to be in the furthest part of the world toward the sunset, there to burn continually" (78).

14 OCTOBER 1728

The horses got some rest by reason of the bad weather, but very little food, the chief of their forage being a little wild rosemary, which resembles the garden rosemary pretty much in figure but not at all in taste or smell. This plant grows in small tufts here and there on the barren land in these upper parts, and the horses liked it well, but the misfortune was, they could not get enough of it to fill their bellies (*H* 250).

Wild rosemary

No such plant is native to the region. Byrd apparently saw a low-growing evergreen shrub with grayish-green leaves and decided it must have been related to the European rosemary so often cultivated in colonial herb gardens. Cumberland rosemary *(Conradia verticillata)* fits the description but is not found here.

15 OCTOBER 1728

The surveyors had much difficulty in getting over the river, finding it deeper than formerly. The breadth of it here did not exceed fifty yards. The banks were about twenty feet high from the water and beautifully beset with canes. Our baggage horses crossed not the river here at all but, fetching a compass, went round the bent of it. On our way we forded Sable Creek, so called from the dark color of the water, which happened, I suppose, by its being shaded on both sides with canes.

In the evening we quartered in a charming situation near the angle of the river, from whence our eyes were carried down both reaches, which kept a straight course for a great way together. This prospect was so beautiful that we were perpetually climbing up to a neighboring eminence that we might enjoy it in more perfection.

Now the weather grew cool, the wild geese began to direct their flight this way from Hudson's Bay and the lakes that lay northwest of us. They are very lean at their first coming but fatten soon upon a sort of grass that grows on the shores and rocks of this river. The Indians call this fowl "cohunks," from the hoarse note it has, and begin the year from the coming of the cohunks, which happens in the beginning of October. These wild geese are guarded from cold by a down that is exquisitely soft and fine, which makes them much more valuable for their feathers than for their flesh, which is dark and coarse (*H* 250).

Sable Creek

Sable Creek has lost its name. Byrd may refer to what is now Williamson Creek, located a few miles west of Danville in a bend in the river. The river is fairly deep and has steep banks all through this section.

I believe the campsite was located just beyond Williamson Creek, between Williamson and White Oak Creeks, on high ground overlooking the Dan. The general area is accessible now only from the North Carolina side of the river, on the Gravel Hill Road.

Wild geese

Migrating geese used the Dan River for centuries, but during the 1960s the development of large farming operations in the Northeast and the Middle Atlantic States began "short stopping" geese. That is, geese that had migrated to wintering grounds in the Southeast, finding plenty of available food in the huge, harvested fields further north, simply wintered over in more northerly areas. This section of Virginia and North Carolina gets almost no migrating Canada geese now, but it does have a fairly large population of resident geese, birds that no longer migrate long distances north and south. Many of these birds continue to use the Dan River, but they are more apt to fatten up by feeding in local grainfields or even on golf courses than by eating "a sort of grass that grows on the shores and rocks of this river."

16 OCTOBER 1728

The high land we traveled over was very good, and the low grounds promised the greatest fertility of any I had ever seen. At the end of 4 miles and 311 poles from where we lay, the line intersected the Dan the fifth time. We had day enough to carry it farther, but the surveyors could find no safe ford over the river. This obliged us to ride two miles up the river in quest of a ford, and by the way we traversed several small Indian fields, where we conjectured the Sauros had been used to plant corn, the town where they had lived lying seven or eight miles more southerly upon the eastern side of the river. These Indian fields produced a sweet kind of grass, almost knee-high, which was excellent forage for the horses. . . .

The trees grew surprisingly large in this low ground, and among the rest we observed a tall kind of hickory, peculiar to the upper parts of the country. It is covered with a very rough bark and produces a nut with a thick shell that is easily broken. The kernel is not so rank as that of the common hickory but altogether as oily. . . .

The Indian killed a fat buck, and the men brought in four bears and a brace of wild turkeys, so that this was truly a land of plenty both for man and beast (*H* 251–52).

Sauros

The Sauro Indians had lived just south of the Dan for years before Byrd made his journey, and he knew of them through Indian traders. (Sauraton Mountain, in Stokes County, North Carolina, is named for the tribe.) By 1728, however, most of the Sauros had fled further south to avoid raiding parties from Seneca/Iroquois tribes traveling through the area. They were soon incorporated into other tribes and disappeared as a separate entity.

"A tall kind of hickory"

The shagbark or shellbark hickory *(Carya ovata)* is encountered in the area, but not as frequently as the bitternut hickory *(C. cordiformis),* the mockernut hickory *(C. tomentosa),* and other smooth-barked hickory trees.

"A land of plenty"

Though concentrating chiefly on the plentiful wildlife of the area and on its natural beauty, Byrd was also very taken with the idea that it would make valuable and productive farmland for English settlers. Accordingly, he returned to the area later and managed to acquire some twenty thousand acres of land just a little to the south and west of the spot he describes in this paragraph. He called the area "the land of Eden." There is now a small town there, in northern Rockingham County, North Carolina, located on and around the land Byrd acquired. The name of the town is Eden.

17 OCTOBER 1728

We detached a party of men this morning early in search of a ford, who after all could find none that was safe; though, dangerous as it was, we determined to make use of it to avoid all farther delay. Accordingly we rode over a narrow ledge of rocks, some of which lay below the surface and some above it. Those that lay under the water were slippery as ice; and the current glided over them so swiftly that though it was only water it made us perfectly drunk. Yet we were all so fortunate as to get safe over to the west shore with no other damage than the sopping some of our bread by the flouncing of the horses. The tedious time spent in finding out this ford and in getting all the horses over it prevented our carrying the line more than 2 miles and 250 poles.

This was the last time we crossed the Dan with our line, which now began to run away more southerly with a very flush

and plentiful stream, the description whereof must be left to future discoveries, though we are well assured by the Indians that
it runs through the mountains. . . .

We marked out our quarters on the banks of a purling stream,
which we called Cascade Creek by reason of the multitude of
waterfalls that are in it. But, different from all other falls that
ever I met with, the rocks over which the water rolled were soft
and would split easily into broad flakes, very proper for pavement; and some of it seemed soft enough for hones and the grain
fine enough.

Near our camp we found a prickly shrub rising about a foot
from the ground, something like that which bears the barberry
though much smaller. The leaves had a fresh, agreeable smell,
and I am persuaded the ladies would be apt to fancy a tea made
of them, provided they were told how far it came and at the
same time were obliged to buy it very dear (*H* 252–53).

"It runs through the mountains"

The Dan River originates in the mountains near the Blue Ridge
Parkway in Virginia, not very far north and west of where Byrd's survey ended. From its origin it flows southward into North Carolina,
then generally northward and eastward until it crosses back into Virginia at the point Byrd describes here.

Cascade Creek

The creek, which still bears its name, enters the Dan River just
south of the line, near Eden. It is an attractive little stream, and the
rocks Byrd describes as "soft" and splitting "easily into broad flakes,
very proper for pavement" are black slate.

"A prickly shrub"

The shrub is probably the American barberry *(Berberis canadensis)*.
Byrd would have been familiar with the European barberry, often
planted as an ornamental hedge, to which the American version is very
similar. Harvill describes its occurrence in Virginia as "infrequent" (74).
Radford et al. note the presence of *B. canadensis* in Caswell County,

North Carolina (*Atlas* 47). Byrd would have been just north and a little west of this area on 17 October. European barberry, *B. vulgaris,* which has since been naturalized in this country, was used in folk medicine, usually for the preparation of a "blood tonic." This probably explains Byrd's interest in the little plant.

18 OCTOBER 1728

We crossed Cascade Creek over a ledge of smooth rocks and then scuffled through a mighty thicket at least three miles long. The whole was one continued tract of rich high land, the woods whereof had been burnt not long before. It was then overgrown with saplings of oak, hickory, and locust, interlaced with grapevines. In this fine land, however, we met with no water, till at the end of three miles we luckily came upon a crystal stream which, like some lovers of conversation, discovered everything committed to its faithless bosom. Then we came upon a piece of rich low ground, covered with large trees, of the extent of half a mile, which made us fancy ourselves not far from the river; though after that we ascended gently to higher land, with no other trees growing upon it except butterwood, which is one species of white maple. . . .

The Indian killed a very fat doe and came across a bear, which had been put to death and was half devoured by a panther. The last of these brutes reigns absolute monarch of the woods and in the keenness of his hunger will venture to attack a bear; though then 'tis ever by surprise, as all beasts of the cat kind use to come upon their prey. Their play is to take the poor bears napping, they being very drowsy animals, and though they be exceedingly strong yet their strength is heavy, while the panthers are too nimble and cunning to trust themselves within their hug. As formidable as this beast is to his fellow brutes, he never hath the confidence to venture upon a man but retires from him with great respect, if there be a way open for his escape. However it must be confessed his voice is a little contemptible for a monarch of the forest, being not a great deal louder nor more awful than the mewing of a household cat. Some authors who

have given an account of the southern continent of America
would make the world believe there are lions; but in all likeli-
hood they were mistaken, imagining these panthers to be lions.
What makes this probable is that the northern and southern
parts of America being joined by the Isthmus of Darien, if there
were lions in either they would find their way into the other, the
latitudes of each being equally proper for that generous animal.

In South Carolina they call this beast a tiger, though improperly, and so they do in some parts of the Spanish West Indies.
Some of their authors, a little more properly, compliment it with
the name of a leopard. But none of these are the growth of
America, that we know of. . . .

From the top of every hill we could discern distinctly, at a
great distance to the northward, three or four ledges of mountains, rising one above another, and on the highest of all rose
a single mountain, very much resembling a woman's breast
(*H* 254−56).

"Butterwood, which is one species of white maple"

Byrd is probably referring to the sycamore tree *(Platanus occiden-*
talis), occasionally called the buttonwood. The sycamore is not related
to the white maple, but it does have very hard, white wood, and its
broad leaves somewhat resemble those of the maple. To add to the
confusion, the European tree called the sycamore is related to the
maples, a fact that Byrd may have known, leading him to confound
the unrelated American species with the maples as well.

There is a kind of walnut tree sometimes called butternut or white
walnut *(Juglans cinera),* but Byrd's description makes it plain that he is
not referring to this tree.

Panther

Early colonial writers about the forests and frontier of America often refer to the panther, and later American writers, including Charles
Brockden Brown, James Fenimore Cooper, and Ambrose Bierce, told
hair-raising stories about its ferocity. Byrd's cool analysis is typical of
his eighteenth-century rationalism. He tries to distinguish between

this cat and others, notes that it is called by a variety of names, gives a description, and adds that it poses no threat to man. (A small number of highly publicized incidents involving lions attacking and sometimes killing and eating humans in the American Southwest and British Columbia in the late twentieth century raises some doubt about the last assertion, but probably the cat never regarded people as a preferred prey species—certainly not since the coming of Europeans with their firearms—and authentic records of attacks are very rare.)

The panther (also called cougar, mountain lion, puma, and—though Byrd frets about it—simply lion) probably occupied all the continental United States in the early eighteenth century. Fears of livestock predation contributed to its extirpation from almost all areas east of the Rocky Mountains by the early twentieth century.

A remnant population of cougars holds on in southern Florida and another in Texas. Persistent rumors of panther sightings, however, continue in many eastern and southeastern states, particularly in the Appalachian Mountains and in some of the larger tracts of forest swampland. The Virginia Department of Game and Inland Fisheries investigates cougar sightings every year, the majority of them coming from the mountains of southwest Virginia. Most of North Carolina's sightings (investigated by the North Carolina Wildlife Resources Commission) come from the area around the Great Smoky Mountains National Park and from some of the eastern counties. The U.S. Fish and Wildlife Service lists "known occurrences" in eight counties in North Carolina. However, a cautionary note in its *Endangered and Threatened Species of the Southeastern United States,* summarizing the results of a five-year survey that attempted to determine the presence of a self-sustaining cougar population in the Southern Appalachians, says that no "concrete evidence" of eastern cougar populations was obtained, despite many promising leads.

Concrete evidence would be dead or trapped cougars or absolutely incontrovertible evidence in the form of videotapes and scat. So far, no one has been able to come up with much of this kind of evidence. Two cougars killed in eastern North Carolina, in Tyrrell County, in the 1980s proved to be imports from a western state. Whether similar imports could have reestablished resident populations or the secretive

nature of the great cats has allowed a remnant population of the original eastern subspecies to persist in some wilderness areas remains to
be seen. In order to safeguard what may or may not be a genuine population of the animals, both North Carolina and Virginia have declared the cougar a protected species, as have twenty-two other states
in the historical range of the eastern cougar.

"Three or four ledges of mountains"

The party was looking toward Turkeycock Mountain, which rises
sharply from the rolling hills of Henry County, Virginia, about twenty
miles north of the line.

19 OCTOBER 1728

About four miles beyond the river Irvin we forded Matrimony
Creek, called so by an unfortunate married man because it was
exceedingly noisy and impetuous. However, though the stream
was clamorous, yet like those women who make themselves
plainest heard, it was likewise perfectly clear and unsullied. Still
half a mile farther we saw a small mountain about five miles to
the northwest of us, which we called the Wart because it appeared no bigger than a wart in comparison of the great mountains which hid their haughty heads in the clouds. . . .

The men's mouths watered at the sight of a prodigious flight
of wild pigeons, which flew high over our heads to the southward. The flocks of these birds of passage are so amazingly great
sometimes that they darken the sky, nor is it uncommon for
them to light in such numbers in the larger limbs of mulberry
trees and oaks as to break them down. In their travels they make
vast havoc amongst the acorns and berries of all sorts that they
waste whole forests in a short time and leave a famine behind
them for most other creatures; and under some trees where they
light, it is no strange thing to find the ground covered three
inches thick with their dung. These wild pigeons commonly
breed in the uninhabited parts of Canada and as the cold approaches assemble their armies and bend their course southerly,
shifting for their quarters, like many of the winged kind, accord-

ing to the season. But the most remarkable thing in their flight, we are told, is that they never have been observed to return to the northern countries the same way they came from thence but take another route, I suppose for better subsistence. In these long flights they are very lean and their flesh is far from being white or tender, though good enough upon a march, when hunger is the sauce and makes it go down better than truffles and morels do (*H* 257).

Matrimony Creek

Matrimony Creek kept its name. It twists through northern Rockingham County, North Carolina, and southern Henry County, Virginia, crossing the state line twice between Eden and U.S. 220, south of Martinsville. The creek empties into the Dan just below the town of Eden, but of course Byrd did not get quite that far south. He knew only that the river appeared to drop southward and to have its origin "in the southern mountains."

"Which we called the Wart"

The mountain referred to here is Chestnut Knob, about five miles north of the line and five miles south of Martinsville, Virginia.

"A prodigious flight of wild pigeons"

Incredible as it may seem, the now-extinct passenger pigeon of North America may once have been the most numerous bird on earth. Estimates of its total population run to over 5 billion birds. Eyewitness accounts of the birds traveling in flocks of over a million, which darkened the sky and took several hours to pass, are commonplace in the late seventeenth and early eighteenth centuries.

Passenger pigeons were about the size of mourning doves, which they closely resembled. Like doves, they had elongated, slender tails and flew very rapidly. Their upper surfaces had a bluish color, unlike the soft gray of the mourning dove. Females laid one egg at a time, with two single-egg clutches in a year. The birds ranged as far north as Canada in the summer, and they wintered in the southern United States.

Market hunters decimated large numbers of passenger pigeons in the eighteenth century, but what contributed at least as much to the quick demise of the species was the clearing of the forests. The pigeons nested in large blocks of forest, and when the large blocks became fewer and fewer, the birds became, of necessity, more concentrated. This exacerbated problems caused by disease, parasites, predators, and hunters. As ever more American forest land was cleared, the population of passenger pigeons dropped quickly. Unlike many other species, this one had almost vanished before the early days of conservation movements. By the late 1800s there were almost no passenger pigeons left, except for a few specimens in zoos. When the second decade of the twentieth century had ended, there were none at all.

20 OCTOBER 1728

It was now Sunday, which we had like to have spent in fasting as well as in prayer; for our men, taking no care for the morrow, like good Christians but bad travelers, had improvidently devoured all their meat for supper. They were ordered in the morning to drive up their horses, lest they should stray too far from the camp and be lost in case they were let alone all day. At their return they had the very great comfort to behold a monstrous fat bear, which the Indian had killed very seasonably for their breakfast. We thought it still necessary to make another reduction of our bread, from four to three pounds a week to every man, computing that we had still enough in that proportion to last us three weeks longer.

The atmosphere was so smoky all round us that the mountains were again grown invisible. This happened not from the haziness of the sky but from the firing of the woods by the Indians, for we were now near the route the northern savages take when they go out to war against the Catawbas and other southern nations. On their way, the fires they make in their camps are left burning, which, catching the dry leaves that lie near, soon put the adjacent woods into a flame. Some of our men in search of their horses discovered one of these Indian camps, where not long before they had been a-furring and dressing their skins.

And now I mention the northern Indians, it may not be improper to take notice of their implacable hatred to those of the south. Their wars are everlasting, without any peace, enmity being the only inheritance among them that descends from father to son, and either party will march a thousand miles to take revenge upon such hereditary enemies (*H* 257–58).

"The firing of the woods by Indians"

Byrd mentions frequently during the next several days the smoke from fires set by Indians. He is concerned both because the fires might burn the vegetation off the ground through which the party must pass, leaving the horses hungry, and because of the very real danger of encountering a large raiding party.

The Northern Indians

The relationship between the Tuscarora, a tribe that was by now in league with other Iroquoian tribes in the Northeast, and the Catawba tribe, whose lands lay to the south of Byrd's march, has already been described in chapter 2. The near extermination of the North Carolina branch of the Tuscaroras by the white settlers and their Catawba allies was cause for continued warfare well into the eighteenth century.

Byrd discourses at length upon Indian methods of warfare; the practice of scalping (for which he finds precedence among "the ancient Scythians" and to which he compares the Old Testament practice of taking the foreskins of Philistines); and the various methods of torturing enemies, pointing out that the cruelest punishments were often reserved for the most noble captives. Lest his readers regard the Native Americans as having a corner on the market for ingenious torture of distinguished enemies, however, Byrd reminds us that our own famous heroes have been guilty of as much cruelty: "Though who can reproach the poor Indians for this, when Homer makes his celebrated hero, Achilles, drag the body of Hector at the tail of his chariot for having fought gallantly in defense of his country? Nor was Alexander the Great, with all his famed generosity, less inhuman to the brave Tyrians, two thousand of which he ordered to be crucified in cold

blood for no other fault but for having defended their city most coura-
geously against him during a siege of seven months" (*H* 260).

21 OCTOBER 1728

The apprehensions we had of losing the horses in these copse-
woods were too well founded, nor were the precautions we used
yesterday of driving them up sufficient to prevent their straying
away afterwards, notwithstanding they were securely hobbled.
We therefore ordered the men out early this morning to look
diligently for them, but it was late before any could be found. It
seems they had straggled in quest of forage, and, besides all that,
the bushes grew thick enough to conceal them from being seen
at the smallest distance. One of the people was so bewildered in
search of his horse that he lost himself, being no great forester.
However, because we were willing to save time, we left two of
our most expert woodsmen behind to beat all the adjacent
woods in quest of him. . . .

The smoke continued still to veil the mountains from our
sight, which made us long for rain or a brisk gale of wind to dis-
perse it. Nor was the loss of this wild prospect all our concern,
but we were apprehensive lest the woods should be burnt in the
course of our line before us or happen to take fire behind us,
either of which would effectually have starved the horses and
made us all foot soldiers. But we were so happy, thank God,
as to escape this misfortune in every part of our progress.

We were exceedingly uneasy about our lost man, knowing he
had taken no provision of any kind, nor was it much advantage
toward his support that he had taken his gun along with him,
because he had rarely been guilty of putting anything to death.
He had unluckily wandered from the camp several miles, and after steering sundry unsuccessful courses in order to return either
to us or to the line, was at length so tired he could go no farther.
In this distress he sat himself down under a tree to recruit his
jaded spirits and at the same time indulge a few melancholy
reflections. Famine was the first phantom that appeared to him

and was the more frightful because he fancied himself not quite bear enough to subsist long upon licking his paws. In the meantime, the two persons we had sent after him hunted diligently great part of the day without coming upon his track. They fired their pieces toward every point of the compass but could perceive no firing in return. However, advancing a little farther, at last they made a lucky shot that our straggler had the good fortune to hear, and, he returning the salute, they soon found each other with no small satisfaction. But though they light of the man, they could by no means light of his horse, and therefore he was obliged to be a foot soldier all the rest of the journey.

Our Indian shot a bear so prodigiously fat that there was no way to kill him but by firing in his ear. The fore part of the skull of that animal, being guarded by a double bone, is hardly penetrable, and when it is very fat, a bullet aimed at his body is apt to lose its force before it reaches the vitals. The animal is of the dog kind, and our Indian, as well as woodsmen, are as fond of its flesh as the Chinese can be of that of the common hound (*H* 260–62).

"Being no great forester"

The lost man, identified in *The Secret History* as George Hamilton, managed to get lost a second time a few days later.

"Licking his paws"

Byrd refers to a misconception attributed to Sir John Mandeville that a bear could live for a time merely by licking its paws.

"Of the dog kind"

Byrd suggests here and elsewhere that bears are somehow related to dogs. (They are not.) His observation about the fondness of the men for bear meat is repeated several times in *The History* and *The Secret History*. See especially his descriptions of Reverend Fontaine "growling like a wildcat over a squirrel" while eating bear meat.

22 OCTOBER 1728

As we rode along we found no less than three bears and a fat
doe, that our Indian, who went out before us, had thrown in our
course, and we were very glad to pick them up. About a mile
from the camp we crossed Miry Creek, so called because several
of the horses were mired in its branches. About 230 poles beyond that, the line intersected another river that seemed to be a
branch of the Irvin, to which we gave the name of the Mayo in
compliment to the other of our surveyors. It was about fifty
yards wide where we forded it and made a natural cascade. Our
horses could hardly keep their feet over these slippery rocks,
which gave some of their riders no small palpitation. This river
forks about a quarter of a mile below the ford and has some
scattering canes growing near the mouth of it.

We pitched our tent on the western banks of the Mayo, for
the pleasure of being lulled to sleep by the cascade. Here our
hunters had leisure to go out and try their fortunes, and returned
loaded with spoil. They brought in no less than six bears, exceedingly fat, so that the frying pan had no rest all night. . . .
These beasts always endeavor to avoid a man, except they are
wounded or happen to be engaged in the protection of their
cubs. By the force of these instincts and that of self-preservation,
they will now and then throw off all reverence for their Maker's
image. For that reason, excess of hunger will provoke them
to the same desperate attack for the support of their being
(*H* 262–63).

"Which we gave the name of the Mayo"

The Mayo River crosses the line near the southwestern corner of
Henry County, Virginia. It runs into the Dan River about eleven miles
further south, at Madison-Mayodan, North Carolina.

"These beasts always endeavor to avoid a man"

Here again, Byrd is anxious to clear up misconceptions about
bears and other animals. Despite its fearsome reputation among some
writers of frontier fiction, the black bear rarely attacks human beings.

Wounded bears, or sow bears protecting cubs, have injured and killed humans, and there are a few recorded cases of black bears stalking, killing, and devouring people. Most such instances in recent years have involved young male bears that are establishing themselves in new territory. In a highly publicized incident in Great Smoky Mountains National Park, on 21 May 2000, a small sow bear and her half-grown cub killed and partially ate a woman hiker. Still, such incidents are extremely rare, and Byrd's characterization of black bears as anxious to avoid encounters with humans is correct. Until the death of the woman in 2000, there had never been a human fatality attributable to a bear attack in the park, despite the very large number of tourists and hikers who share the park with over 1,800 bears every year.

23 OCTOBER 1728

At the distance of sixty-two poles from where we lay, we crossed the south branch of what we took for the Irvin, nor was it without difficulty we got over, though it happened to be without damage. Great part of the way after that was mountainous, so that we were no sooner got down one hill but we were obliged to climb up another. Only for the last mile of our stage we encountered a locust thicket, that was level but interlaced terribly with briars and grapevines. We forded a large creek no less than five times, the banks of which were so steep that we were forced to cut them down with a hoe. We gave it the name of Crooked Creek because of its frequent meanders. . . .

The mountains were still concealed from our eyes by a cloud of smoke. As we went along we were alarmed at the sight of a great fire which showed itself to the northward. This made our small corps march in closer order than we used to do, lest perchance we might be waylaid by Indians. It made us look out sharp to see if we could discover any track or other token of these insidious foresters, but found none. In the meantime, we came upon the track of bears, which can't without some skill be distinguished from that of human creatures made with naked feet. And, indeed, a young woodsman would be puzzled to find out the difference, which consists principally in a bear's paws

being something smaller than a man's foot and in its leaving
sometimes the mark of its claws in the impression made upon
the ground.

The soil where the locust thicket grew was exceedingly rich,
as it constantly is where that kind of tree is naturally and largely
produced. But the desolation made there lately, either by fire or
caterpillars, had been so general that we could not see a tree of
any bigness standing within our prospect. . . .

There is a beautiful range of hills, as level as a terrace walk,
that overlooks the valley through which Crooked Creek conveys
its spiral stream. This terrace runs pretty near east and west
about two miles south of the line and is almost parallel with it.
The horses had been too much harassed to permit us to ride
at all out of our way for the pleasure of any prospect or the
gratification of any curiosity. This confined us to the narrow
sphere of our business and is at the same time a just excuse for
not animating our story with greater variety (*H* 263–65).

"A locust thicket"

There are two kinds of locust trees frequently encounted in the
area—the black locust *(Robinia pseudoacacia)* and the honey locust
(Gleditsia triacanthos). Both have formidable thorns, with those of the
former being short and hooked and those of the latter being very long
and growing in groups of two or three. Either would impede the
progress of a survey party.

According to Harvill (130), black locust trees tend to grow thickly
in recently burned-over areas such as the one Byrd describes here.
Black locust is particularly valuable for its ability to resist rot, and
farmers often use it for fence posts or for making log barns.

"The track of bears"

The rear foot of a black bear does make a track closely resembling
that of a barefoot human. The front foot, on the other hand, has a much
more rounded shape. It somewhat resembles the print one might make
if he put the heel and palm of the hand to the ground, curling the

fingers under, then drew claw marks beyond the edges of the marks left by the curled-under fingers. I have rarely seen the track of only the rear foot of a bear.

24 OCTOBER 1728

The line was extended six miles and three hundred poles and in that distance crossed Crooked Creek at least eight times more. We were forced to scuffle through a thicket about two miles in breadth, planted with locusts and hickory saplings as close as they could stand together. Amongst these there was hardly a tree of tolerable growth within view. It was a dead plain of several miles extent and very fertile soil. Beyond that the woods were open for about three miles but mountainous. All the rest of our day's journey was pestered with bushes and grapevines, in the thickest of which we were obliged to take up our quarters near one of the branches of Crooked Creek.

This night it was the men's good fortune to fare very sumptuously. The Indian had killed two large bears, the fattest of which he had taken napping. One of the people, too, shot a raccoon, which is also of the dog kind and as big as a small fox, though its legs are shorter and when fat has a much higher relish than either mutton or kid. 'Tis naturally not carnivorous but very fond of Indian corn and persimmons. The fat of this animal is reckoned very good to assuage swellings and inflammations. Some old maids are at the trouble of breeding them up tame for the pleasure of seeing them play over as many humorous tricks as a monkey. It climbs up small trees, like a bear, by embracing the bodies of them (*H* 265–66).

"One of the people, too, shot a raccoon"

Like the bear, the raccoon *(Procyon lotor)* played a valuable role in feeding and clothing early settlers. The meat is dark but flavorful, as Byrd notes, and the animals were (and still are) very plentiful all along the line. Furthermore, the pelts of the raccoon were prized for making warm garments. Raccoons are omnivores, as bears are, and to some people they look vaguely like small bears. Perhaps that is why Byrd lumped bears and raccoons together as being "of the dog kind." (Neither, of course, is related to the dog.)

25 OCTOBER 1728

The air clearing up this morning, we were again agreeably surprised with a full prospect of the mountains. They discovered themselves both to the north and south of us on either side, not distant above ten miles, according to our best computation. We could now see those to the north rise in four distinct ledges one above another, but those to the south formed only a single ledge and that broken and interrupted in many places, or rather they were only single mountains detached from each other. One of the southern mountains was so vastly high it seemed to hide its head in the clouds, and the west end of it terminated in a horrible precipice that we called the Despairing Lover's Leap. The next to it, toward the east, was lower except at one end, where it heaved itself up in the form of a vast stack of chimneys. The course of the northern mountains seemed to tend west-southwest and those to the southward very near west. We could descry other mountains ahead of us, exactly in the course of the line though at a much greater distance. In this point of view, the ledges on the right and left both seemed to close and form a natural amphitheater. Thus 'twas our fortune to be wedged in betwixt these two ranges of mountains, insomuch that if our line had run ten miles on either side it had butted before this day either upon one or the other, both of them now stretching away plainly to the eastward of us.

It had rained a little in the night, which dispersed the smoke and opened this romantic scene to us all at once, though it was again hid from our eyes as we moved forward by the rough woods we had the misfortune to be engaged with. The bushes were so thick for near four miles together that they tore the deerskins to pieces that guarded the bread bags. Though, as rough as the woods were, the soil was extremely good all the way, being washed down from the neighboring hills into the

plain country. Notwithstanding all these difficulties, the surveyors drove on the line 4 miles and 225 poles. . . .

We saw very few squirrels in the upper parts, because the
wildcats devour them unmercifully. Of these there are four kinds:
the fox squirrel, the gray, the flying, and the ground squirrel.
These last resemble a rat in everything but the tail and the black
and russet streaks that run down the length of their little bodies
(*H* 266–67).

"A full prospect of the mountains"

From this vantage point Byrd could now clearly see the Blue Ridge
range to the west and north. Less than ten miles to the north is No
Business Mountain, and a little to the west of that, Bull Mountain—
both of them fairly impressive peaks. Beyond No Business Mountain
rise various knobs and peaks in the Blue Ridge Mountains of Patrick
County, Virginia.

Byrd's position was almost due north of Hanging Rock State Park,
in Stokes County, North Carolina. Looking directly southward, he
would have seen the sheer rock walls at the west face of the mountain
and (more impressive in appearance) the huge cliff on the west face of
Moore's Knob. Moore's Knob is surely the mountain he describes as
"Despairing Lover's Leap." I asked for and received permission to hike
across several fields and woodlots until I had reached what I thought
was almost exactly the spot at which Byrd ended his survey. Looking
directly to the south, as he did, I could see the sheer wall of Moore's
Knob as the most prominent object on the skyline.

To the west of Moore's Knob and Hanging Rock is Sauratown
Mountain, and a few miles west of that, Pilot Mountain, with its distinct dome. All these mountains, rising as they do from the rolling hills
of the Stokes County piedmont, would indeed have appeared to Byrd
as "single mountains detached from each other."

"Of these there are four kinds"

Byrd's ceaseless tendency to categorize information is a mark of
his reading in the sciences of his day, and if he often oversimplifies
or just errs (as in lumping bears and raccoons together as being "of

the dog kind"), he is at least systematic. The fox squirrel he mentions *(Sciurus niger)* is about half again as big as the common gray squirrel *(Sciurus carolinensis)* and tends to be much darker in color. Fox squirrels are much more common now west of the Blue Ridge Mountains of Virginia than in the Piedmont. The southern flying squirrel *(Glaucomys volans)* is frequent all along the line, but it is not frequently seen, being mostly nocturnal and spending much of the day hidden away in hollow trees. Flying squirrels are about half the size of gray squirrels. They do not, of course, fly. The loose membrane along their flanks, near the fore- and hind legs, can be spread out like a sail when they jump from one tree to another, giving the impression that they soar like birds. The "ground squirrel" Byrd describes is the striped chipmunk *(Tamias striatus).*

Squirrels—especially gray and fox squirrels—formed an important part of the daily diet of many frontier families, but Byrd does not mention using them as food. Possibly the sheer number in the party (twenty-six men at this point) and the difficulty of procuring and preparing enough of the small mammals for the table would have made them unsuitable. Furthermore, though the party was occasionally hungry, there was usually a superfluity of other game—from deer to bear to buffalo—from which to choose. While he mentions the men's desire to obtain passenger pigeons for food, the only small mammals he describes as table fare are the raccoon, the opossum, and (surprisingly) the skunk.

26 OCTOBER 1728

We found our way grow still more mountainous, after extending the line three hundred poles farther. We came then to a rivulet that ran with a swift current toward the south. This we fancied to be another branch of the Irvin, though some of these men, who had been Indian traders, judged it rather to be the head of Deep River, that discharges its stream into that of Pee Dee, but this seemed a wild conjecture. The hills beyond that river were exceedingly lofty and not to be attempted by our jaded palfreys, which could by now hardly drag their legs after them upon level ground. Besides, the bread began to grow scanty and the winter season to advance upon us. We had likewise reason to apprehend the consequences of being intercepted by deep snows and the swelling of the many waters between us and home. The first of these misfortunes would starve all our horses and the other ourselves, by cutting off our retreat and obliging us to winter in those desolate woods. These considerations determined us to stop short here and push our adventures no farther. The last tree we marked was a red oak growing on the bank of the river; and to make the place more remarkable, we blazed all the trees around it.

We found the whole distance from Currituck Inlet to the rivulet where we left off to be, in a straight line, 240 miles and 230 poles. And from that place where the Carolina commissioners deserted us, 72 miles and 302 poles. This last part of the journey was generally very hilly, or else grown up with troublesome thickets and underwoods, all which our Carolina friends had the discretion to avoid. We encamped in a dirty valley near the rivulet above-mentioned for the advantage of the canes, and so sacrificed our own convenience to that of our horses. There was a small mountain half a mile to the northward of us, which we had the curiosity to climb up in the afternoon in order to enlarge our prospect. From thence we were able to discover where the two ledges of mountains closed, as near as we could guess about thirty miles to the west of us, and lamented that our present circumstances would not permit us to advance the line to that place, which the hand of Nature had made so very remarkable.

Not far from our quarters one of the men picked up a pair of elk's horns, not very large, and discovered the track of the elk that had shed them. It was rare to find any tokens of those animals so far to the south, because they keep commonly to the northward of thirty-seven degrees, as the buffaloes, for the most part, confine themselves to the southward of that latitude. The elk is full as big as a horse and of the deer kind. The stags only have horns and those exceedingly large and spreading. Their color is something lighter than that of the red deer and their flesh tougher. Their swiftest speed is a large trot, and in that motion they turn their horns back upon their necks and cock their noses aloft in the air. Nature has taught them this attitude to save their antlers from being entangled in the thickets, which they always retire to. They are very shy and have the sense of smelling so exquisite that they wind a man at a great distance. For this reason they are seldom seen but when the air is moist, in which case their smell is not so nice. They commonly herd together, and the Indians say if one of the drove happen by some wound to be disabled in making his escape, the rest will forsake their fears to defend their friend, which they will do with great obstinacy till they are killed upon the spot. Though, otherwise, they are so alarmed at the sight of a man that to avoid him they will sometimes throw themselves down very high precipices into the river. . . .

Our men had the fortune to kill a brace of bears, a fat buck, and a wild turkey, all which paid them with interest for yesterday's abstinence. This constant and seasonable supply of our daily wants made us reflect thankfully on the bounty of Providence. And that we might not be unmindful of being all along fed by Heaven in this great and solitary wilderness, we agreed to wear in our hats the maosti, which is in Indian the beard of a wild turkey cock, and on our breasts the figure of that fowl with its wings extended and holding in its claws a scroll with this motto, Vice coturnicum, meaning that we had been supported by them in the wilderness in the room of quails (*H* 270).

"The head of Deep River"

Byrd was correct in calling this a "wild conjecture." The Deep River rises just west of Greensboro, North Carolina, a good distance to the south of the line. The men were probably on Peters Creek, five miles south of present-day Stuart, Virginia, in Patrick County. Interestingly enough, had they continued the line just six more miles westward, they would have crossed the Dan one more time.

"The whole distance from Currituck Inlet"

In *The Secret History,* Byrd gives the distance as 241½ miles and 70 poles. In a list entitled "The Distances of Places Mentioned in the

Foregoing History of The Dividing Line Between Virginia and North Carolina," the total is 241 miles, 150 poles. The distance given here is just under 241 miles. Wright discusses these discrepancies briefly (*SH* 129).

"Where the Carolina commissioners deserted us"

On 5 October, while the party was camped at Hyco River, the commissioners from North Carolina suddenly announced their intention to leave the survey and go home. Byrd expresses surprise, annoyance, and a little relief at the announcement, the relief coming from the prospect of an end to the nearly continuous quarreling between the two groups. His summary seems a little smug: "But although we were to be so unhappy as to lose the assistance of their great abilities, yet we, who were concerned for Virginia, determined, by the grace of God, not to do our work by halves but, all deserted as were like to be, should think it our duty to push the line quite to the mountains; and if their government should refuse to be bound by so much of the line as was run without their commissioners, yet at least it would bind Virginia and stand as a direction how far His Majesty's lands extend to the southward" (*H* 237). (See also the comments for Byrd's entry on 5 October, in chapter 2.)

In *The Secret History* Byrd includes a document written by the Carolina commissioners explaining their reasons for abandoning the venture. (Briefly, they had determined that they had gone far enough to establish the line. See the discussion in chapter 2.) Noting that the two groups parted with all signs of friendship and good humor, he cannot resist adding a sarcasm: "They took their leave, . . . just like some men and their wives who, after living together all their time in perpetual discord and uneasiness, will yet be very good friends at the point of death when they are sure they shall part forever" (*SH* 112).

"Where the two ledges of mountains closed"

Just over thirty miles from the spot where Byrd made this observation, the mountains of the Blue Ridge rise in a nearly unbroken chain angling from southwest to northeast. Byrd would not be the last to be awed by the sight.

"A pair of elk's horns"

Elk *(Cervus elaphus)* were widely distributed over much of North America before 1800. Market hunting and a rapid loss of habitat severely reduced their numbers in the nineteenth century. Restoration projects and careful conservation and management plans have contributed to raising the number of elk in the wild today to its highest level in a century. Currently, the total elk population on the North American continent is around one million animals, or approximately 10 percent of the population prior to European settlement. The vast majority of these animals live in the Rocky Mountain states, but rapid human encroachment threatens their habitat even there, especially in states such as Colorado, with burgeoning human populations.

A number of eastern and southern states have tried, with mixed success, to reintroduce elk to their former ranges. At this time there are small populations in the wild in Pennsylvania, Kentucky, and Arkansas. Among the problems facing such efforts at reintroduction have been the elks' depredation of farm crops such as alfalfa, competition for natural forage with white-tailed deer, and concerns about the possibility of introducing diseases that might cross to the white-tailed population.

Byrd's comment about the similarities between the American elk and the European red deer are right on target. Many biologists now believe that the ancestors of European and Asian red deer migrated across the Bering Straits land bridge some time before the first humans did, probably around 120,000 years ago. One of the reasons the human hunters came was to follow these red deer.

One of the most interesting points about Byrd's observation is the fact that his men found the antlers in the fall. Elk, like deer, shed their antlers in the late winter or early spring. Mice and other small mammals eat the shed antlers greedily for the calcium in them, and it is fairly unusual (although not unheard of) to find complete "sheds" any later than the spring of the year. Those that are found later in the year are almost always badly gnawed and scarred, and they are rarely found in pairs. Byrd does not comment on the condition of the shed antlers, but he does say that the men found both antlers.

"The beard of a wild turkey cock"

Byrd had earlier referred to this practice when the men named Cockade Creek (now called Country Line Creek). (See his entry for 10 October in *The History* and the comment, with its reference to *The Secret History,* above.) The mature male turkey sports a tuft of specialized, hairlike feathers growing from its chest and hanging down like a beard. This beard may be as much as a foot long in very large birds. It is easily detached from the body of the bird, and both settlers and Native Americans used the brushlike appendage as a decoration and (as here) an ornament on clothing.

The joke about wearing an escutcheon featuring a wild turkey with outstretched wings, bearing a scroll with the motto *vice coturnicum* ("in place of quails"), refers to the Old Testament story of God's providing "flesh" in the form of quails for the people of Israel as they wandered through the desert: "In the evening quails came up and covered the camp; and in the morning dew lay round about the camp" (Exodus 16:13). It would be difficult to imagine a more grotesque-looking coat of arms.

4 ❊ HOMECOMING, HARDSHIPS, AND OBSERVATIONS

BYRD'S PARTY extended the line through 26 October. Then, fearing the onset of cold weather and realizing that they were running low on supplies, they somewhat reluctantly turned around and headed for home. They were tempted, Byrd tells us, to explore a little of the land to the north of the line, to "find whether James River and Appomatox River head there" (*H* 271), but they worried that the first snows of the season might catch them in the mountains. Byrd points out that a thorough exploration of the mountains at the earliest possible date is a necessity for the safety and the prosperity of the colony, and he reminds his readers that the French, who had been in America for a shorter period than the English, were already more familiar with much of the wilderness, especially that to the north and west of Virginia.

Although the retracing of the line on the return trip might seem at first a relatively easy task, the recent rains that had swelled the rivers and the prospect of conflict with northern Indians made it uncertain. Furthermore, there were other animals and plants to record and comment upon, and Byrd discusses more medicinal plants; describes the great fish called the sturgeon; gives his opinions of that curious American marsupial, the opossum; and comments on the reputed powers of a bear-meat diet and of ginseng. He even describes the skunk—both as an animal in the wild and as an item at the table. Byrd seems in high spirits during this portion of the trip. He allows himself the leisure to speculate on the relationship between the animals and plants he sees and those native to other parts of the world, and he ranges widely, covering the llamas and alpacas of South America, the crocodiles of Africa, and the tarantulas of the Old World.

Much of this section of the narrative is given over to conjecture, puffery from the Virginia colony at the expense of the North Carolina one, and anecdotes about various species Byrd either observed or read about. He also discourses on the lands to the south of the line that he had not seen but that he knew about from the reports of other travelers, including Indian traders who had established routes to the lands of the Catawbas and the Cherokees.

Byrd also describes at length the fertility of the lands just south of the line, and we know that he returned in a few years in order to lay claim to several thousand acres of this land. He tells us something more of the history of the Indians in the area, speculates on the future of the colony of Virginia, and describes the river systems reaching from the Roanoke all the way to Cape Fear. In passing he cannot resist making a few more scurrilous comments about the idleness of the inhabitants of North Carolina, which he believes might be an extremely prosperous colony (blessed as it is with such a mild climate and such rich natural resources) but for the intrinsic laziness of its people.

The party crossed the Nottoway River on 20 November and shortly after that reached Sapony Chapel, "which was the first house of prayer [they] had seen for more than two calendar months." Before noon on 22 November, the party disbanded. Byrd ends with a triumphant note: "Thus ended our second expedition, in which we extended the line within the shadow of the Cherokee mountains, where we were obliged to set up our pillars, like Hercules, and return home." He adds that the whole affair had been done with relatively little expense to the Crown, "the whole charge, from beginning to end, amounting to no more than £1,000."

27 OCTOBER 1728

There fell some rain before noon, which made our camp more a bog than it was before. This moist situation began to infect some of the men with fevers and some with fluxes, which however we soon removed with Peruvian bark and ipecacuanha.

In the afternoon we marched up again to the top of the hill to
entertain our eyes a second time with the view of the mountains,
but a perverse fog arose that hid them from our sight. In the
evening we deliberated which way it might be most proper to
return. We had at first intended to cross over at the foot of the
mountains to the head of James River, that we might be able to
describe that natural boundary so far. But, on second thoughts,
we found many good reasons against that laudable design, such
as the weakness of our horses, the scantiness of our bread, and
the near approach of winter. We had cause to believe the way
might be full of hills, and the farther we went toward the north,
the more danger there would be of snow. Such considerations as
these determined us at last to make the best of our way back
upon the line, which was the straightest and consequently the
shortest way to the inhabitants. So prudence got the better for
once of curiosity, and the itch for new discoveries gave place to
self-preservation.

Our inclination was the stronger to cross over according to
the course of the mountains, that we might find out whether
James River and Appomatox River head there or run quite
through them. 'Tis certain that Potomac passes in a large stream
through the main ledge and then divides itself into two considerable rivers. That which stretches away to the northward is
called Cohungaroota and that which flows to the southwest hath
the name Sharantow. . . .

In the meantime, it is strange that our woodsmen have not
had curiosity enough to inform themselves more exactly of these
particulars, and it is stranger still that the government has never
thought it worth the expense of making an accurate survey of
the mountains, that we might be masters of that natural fortifica-
tion before the French, who in some places have settlements not
very distant from it. It therefore concerns His Majesty's service
very nearly and the safety of his subjects in this part of the world
to take possession of so important a barrier in time, lest our
good friends, the French, and the Indians through their means,
prove a perpetual annoyance to these colonies (H 270–72).

"To the head of James River"

The explorers certainly made the right decision here. The James, which winds through much of central and eastern Virginia, runs completely through the Blue Ridge range. Byrd's men would have run out of provisions and into hard weather long before they ever reached the headwaters of the James.

"Divides itself into two considerable waters"

The divide is on the border of the states of Virginia, West Virginia, and Maryland. The southern fork, which flows into the Potomac near Harper's Ferry, is the Shenandoah, which in Byrd's day was called the Sharantow. Byrd did not mean to imply that he wanted to explore the upper reaches of the Potomac, which would have been too far away and had already been charted. He was simply curious to know if the James originated in the mountains or if it, like the Potomac, split off into several "considerable waters."

The French

While the idea of a French threat may seem far-fetched to American readers today, we must remember the long adversarial history of the English and the French. Byrd had been a schoolboy in England when, in 1683, the Monmouth Rebellion (fired partly by fears of a Catholic takeover, partly by fears of French influence on English Catholics) wracked that country. Between 1689 and 1763 England and her colonies fought no fewer than four wars with the French. These were the War of the League of Augsburg, the War of Spanish Succession, the War of Austrian Succession, and, of course, the French and Indian War, which broke out twenty-seven years after Byrd's survey. English colonists in America lived in constant fear of the French for more than half of the eighteenth century, and not until the articles of peace were signed in 1763, ending the French and Indian War, did the colonists cease regarding France as a threat.

A few years later, when the American colonies had decided they no longer needed England to protect them against the French threat, the archenemy became the most important friend, as Franklin and others cultivated the friendship of France, trying to win its support in the

American Revolution. This ironic turn of events, of course, is the part of the American-French connection most familiar to casual students of American history. In 1728 Byrd would have defined himself as an English subject and a resident of Virginia. The idea of being an "American" (as opposed to something else, such as a transplanted English subject loyal to His Majesty) was at least one generation away.

In the light of this very real fear of the French and their influence and power in the New World, it is useful to reexamine Byrd's comments about the English settlers taking Indian wives. He points out that the policy of "the Most Christian King in Canada and Louisiana," encouraging interracial marriage, has worked far better for the French than a more patronizing attitude has worked for the English. Behind this offhand remark, and behind all the remarks he had made earlier about the advisability of the English settlers' taking Indian wives, lies the fear of a war, pitting the French and their Indian allies against the English. And the fear was to prove true, but not in Virginia and not until eleven years after Byrd's death.

28 OCTOBER 1728

Though it may be very difficult to find a certain cure for the gout, yet it is not improbable but some things may ease the pain and shorten the fits of it. And those medicines are most likely to do this that supple the parts and clear the passage through the narrow vessels that are the seat of this cruel disease. Nothing will do this more suddenly than rattlesnake's oil, which will even penetrate the pores of glass when warmed in the sun. It was unfortunate, therefore, that we had not taken out the fat of those snakes we had killed some time before, for the benefit of so useful an experiment as well as for the relief of our fellow traveler. But lately the Seneca rattlesnake root has been discovered in this country, which, being infused in wine and drank morning and evening, has in several instances had a very happy effect upon the gout, and enabled cripples to throw away their crutches and walk several miles, and, what is stranger still, it takes away the pain in half an hour.

Nor was the gout the only disease amongst us that was hard to cure. We had a man in our company who had too voracious a stomach for a woodsman. He eat as much as any other two, but all he swallowed stuck by him till it was carried off by a strong purge. . . . We gave this poor man several purges, which only eased him for the present, and the next day he would grow burly as ever. At last we gave him a moderate dose of ipecacuanha in broth made very salt, which turned all its operation downwards. This had so happy an effect that from that day forward to the end of our journey all his complaints ceased and the passages continued unobstructed (*H* 272–73).

Rattlesnake's oil

One of the commissioners (identified in *The Secret History* as "Meanwell," or William Dandridge) had badly bruised his foot, bringing on "a formal fit of the gout," accompanied by much swelling. Snake oil was thought to have the power to reduce swelling.

Snake oil was for years regarded as a potent medicine, perhaps on the grounds that anything as mysterious and dangerous as a snake must have great powers. Byrd would probably have been familiar with the story of Asclepius, the legendary physician who discovered a way to bring a king's son back from the dead. Asclepius killed a serpent with his staff, but the snake's mate brought a leaf from a certain herb, placed it on the dead serpent's head, and brought the snake back to life. Asclepius used the herb to raise the dead. (The snake coiled around a staff is still the sign of a healer.)

Partly because it sheds its skin and partly because it seems to come and go between two worlds, the upper earth and the land under the earth, the snake was associated in Greek myth with rebirth and eternal life. In Byrd's day and much later, "snake oil" was a common ingredient in patent medicines, supposed to increase the blood flow and strengthen the patient's constitution. There is, of course, nothing in rattlesnake oil that would make it "penetrate the pores of glass when warmed in the sun."

Seneca rattlesnake root

This is the second time Byrd mentions Seneca snakeroot *(Polygala senega),* and he no doubt was on the lookout for a specimen during the journey, though he failed to find it. It has been used for the treatment of pulmonary disorders such as congestion, chronic bronchitis, and asthma. The plant is also a cathartic and diuretic agent, which might explain Byrd's faith in it as a curative for various kinds of swellings. It is not common in the border counties of either state now.

"We gave this poor man several purges"

Especially in *The Secret History,* Byrd explains that it was necessary, from time to time, to give "vomits" and purges to members of the party. He describes ipecacuaha, or "Indian physic," in detail in his entry for 27 September. Root tea made from wild ipecac is an extremely strong laxative. (See the discussion of Byrd's "home remedies" and the general reliance on laxatives in chapter 3.)

29 OCTOBER 1728

Notwithstanding the falling weather, our hunters sallied out in the afternoon and drove the woods in a ring, which was thus performed: from the circumference of a large circle they all marched inward and drove the game toward the center. By this means they shot a brace of fat bears, which came very seasonably, because we had made clean work in the morning and were in danger of dining with St. Anthony, or His Grace Duke Humphrey. But in this expedition the unhappy man who had lost himself once before straggled again so far in pursuit of a deer that he was hurried a second time quite out of his knowledge; and, night coming on before he could recover the camp, he was obliged to lie down without any of the comforts of fire, food, or covering; nor would his fears suffer him to sleep very sound, because, to his great disturbance, the wolves howled all that night and panthers screamed most frightfully.

In the evening a brisk northwester swept all the clouds from the sky and exposed the mountains as well as the stars to our prospect. That which was the most lofty to the southward and which we called the Lover's Leap, some of our Indian traders fondly fancied was the Kiawan Mountain, which they had formerly seen from the country of the Cherokees. They were the more positive by reason of the prodigious precipice that remarkably distinguished the west end of it. We seemed not to be far enough south for that, though 'tis not improbable but a few miles farther the course of our line might carry us to the most northerly towns of the Cherokees (*H* 273–74).

"Dining with St. Anthony, or His Grace Duke Humphrey"

Both expressions mean to go hungry. (See Wright's explanation in the footnote on page 273 of the *History*.)

"The unhappy man who had lost himself"

The unhappy man was George Hamilton again. While Byrd treats the matter humorously in *The History*, in *The Secret History*, which was written first, he expresses genuine concern: "We fired at least a dozen guns to direct him by their report to our camp, but all in vain: we could get no tidings of him. I was much concerned lest a disaster might befall him, being alone in that doleful wilderness."

Kiawan Mountain

Wright agrees with an earlier biographer who identifies this as Pilot Mountain, approximately twenty miles to the southwest of their position on the 29th. (The name is given as Katawa Mountain in *The Secret History*.) Closer to them and more directly southward would have been Hanging Rock and the high cliffs of Moore's Knob. Moore's Knob exactly fits the description and the location given in Byrd's entry, being almost due south of their position on the 29th and having a very large cliff on its western face. The cliff is even plainly visible from U.S. 58, several miles north of the line and a little east of the town of Stuart. As I explained in chapter 3, when I went to the spot where Byrd stood and looked in the same direction he had looked, I saw that Moore's Knob fits the description better than do any of the other

mountains named above. I believe this must have been what Byrd called
the "Despairing Lover's Leap." Interestingly, there is another cliff to
the north of Stuart now called Lover's Leap, though Byrd never saw it.

30 OCTOBER 1728

Four men were dispatched early to clear the road, that our lame
commissioner's leg might be in less danger of being bruised and
that the baggage horses might travel with less difficulty and
more expedition. As we passed along, by favor of a serene sky
we had still from every eminence a perfect view of the mountains, as well to the north as to the south. We could not forbear
now and then facing about to survey them, as if unwilling to
part with a prospect which at the same time, like some rakes,
was very wild and agreeable. We encouraged the horses to exert
the little strength they had and, being light, they made a shift to
jog on about seven miles.

We encamped on Crooked Creek near a thicket of canes. In
the front of our camp rose a very beautiful hill that bounded our
view at about a mile's distance, and all the intermediate space
was covered with green canes. . . .

In the evening one of the men knocked down an opossum,
which is a harmless little beast that will seldom go out of your
way, and if you take hold of it will only grin and hardly ever
bite. The flesh was well tasted and tender, approaching nearest
to pig, which it also resembled in bigness. The color of its fur
was a goose gray, with swine's snout and a tail like a rat, but at
least a foot long. By twisting this tail about the arm of a tree, it
will hang with all its weight and swing to anything it wants to
take hold of. It has five claws on the forefeet of equal length, but
the hinder feet have only four claws and a sort of thumb standing off at a proper distance. Their feet, being thus formed, qual-
ify them for climbing up trees to catch little birds, which they
are very fond of. But the greatest particularity of this creature,
and which distinguishes it from most others that we are acquainted with, is the false belly of the female, into which her
young retreat in time of danger. She can draw this slit, which is

the inlet into this pouch, so close that you must look narrowly to find it, especially if she happen to be a virgin. Within the false belly may be seen seven or eight teats, on which the young ones grow from their first formation till they are big enough to fall off like ripe fruit from a tree. This is so odd a method of generation that I should not have believed it without the testimony of mine own eyes. Besides, a knowing and credible person has assured me he has more than once observed the embryo opossums growing to the teat before they were completely shaped, and afterwards watched their daily growth till they were big enough for birth. And all this he could the more easily pry into because the dam was so perfectly gentle and harmless that he could handle her just as he pleased.

I could hardly persuade myself to publish a thing so contrary to the course that nature takes in the production of other animals unless it were a matter commonly believed in all countries where that creature is produced and has been often observed by persons of undoubted credit and understanding. They say that the leather-winged bats produce their young in the same uncommon manner; and that young sharks at sea and young vipers ashore run down the throats of their dams when they are closely pursued (*H* 277).

Opossum

Byrd is obviously fascinated and perplexed by this animal *(Didelphis virginiana),* and he means to intrigue his readers. Being a marsupial, it is unlike anything else he has ever encountered or even read about, and it would surely seem even more strange to his readers in England. Still, it looks familiar enough—certainly no more strange and alien than a raccoon or a bear. He can find no way to compare this little animal with what he already knows about other species, though he tries. Byrd obviously thinks the young opossums are born in the pouch. Actually, the mother opossum places them in her pouch after they are born in the normal manner. (It is highly doubtful, then, that a young opossum, "if she happen to be a virgin," would have a slit so tight and difficult to find that "you must look narrowly to find it." The pouch and its attendant slit are only prominent if the female is nursing young; lack of prominence has nothing directly to do with marsupial virginity.)

His comment about the animal's preference for small birds, which it pursues in the treetops, is also mistaken. Opossums are omnivorous, and they are scavenging opportunists. They will certainly eat baby birds, but they are unlikely to catch enough adult birds of any species to sustain them. They feed on vegetable matter and often on carrion.

In casting about for other examples of strange behavior in the rearing of young, Byrd mentions bats, sharks, and snakes. Probably he is trying here to make the opossum seem a little less outlandish. Baby bats will cling tightly to their mother's fur, but bats are not marsupials and lack a pouch. It is true that crocodilian mothers will carry their offspring in their mouths, transporting them from the nest to the relative safety of the water, but sharks do nothing of the kind. Stories about infant serpents fleeing to the safety of their parents' jaws are old, and Byrd would surely have known Edmund Spenser's allegorical serpent, Error, whose offspring creep into her mouth.

Opossums (locally called possums) are numerous all over the Southeast. They are not as often used for food as they once were. Most recipes call for penning the animal up and feeding it a vegetable diet for a week or more before preparing it for the table. Byrd's Virginia readers would probably have known what an opossum looked like, but he was interested in tailoring the account in *The History* to a different audience, perhaps one that included members of the Royal Society back in England. (See the discussion following Byrd's entry for 5 November, below, for more on the differences between the descriptions of events and facts in *The Secret History* and *The History*.)

31 OCTOBER 1728

In the evening we pitched our tent near Miry Creek, though an uncomfortable place to lodge in, purely for the advantage of the canes. Our hunters killed a large doe and two bears, which made all other misfortunes easy. Certainly no Tartar ever loved horse flesh or Hottentot guts and garbage better than woodsmen do bear. The truth of it is, it may be proper food perhaps for such as work or ride it off, but, with our chaplain's leave, who loved it much, I think it not a very proper diet for saints, because 'tis apt to make them a little too rampant. And, now, for the good of mankind and for the better peopling an infant colony, which has no want but that of inhabitants, I will venture to publish a secret of importance which our Indian disclosed to me. I asked him the reason why few or none of his countrywomen were barren. To which curious question he answered, with a broad grin upon his face, they had an infallible secret for that. Upon my being importunate to know what the secret might be, he informed me that if any Indian woman did not prove with child at a decent time after marriage, the husband, to save his reputation with the women, forthwith entered into a bear diet for six weeks, which in that time makes him so vigorous that he grows exceedingly impertinent to his poor wife, and 'tis great odds but he makes her a mother in nine months. And thus much I am able to say besides for the reputation of the bear diet, that all the married men of our company were joyful fathers within forty weeks after they got home, and most of the single men had children sworn to them within the same time, our chaplain always excepted, who, with much ado, made a shift to cast out that importunate kind of devil by dint of fasting and prayer (*H* 278).

Near Miry Creek

Byrd mentions fighting the steep terrain and tangled thickets near Crooked Creek several times as that body of water winds above and below the dividing line. The party would have crossed it, having to ascend and descend its steep banks, at least four times. Their campsite was just east of the present Henry County/Patrick County line, in Virginia, or at the extreme northeast corner of Stokes County, North Carolina.

"I think it not a very proper diet for saints"

Byrd is having fun with the chaplain of the group, Reverend Peter Fontaine, whom he calls "Dr. Humdrum" in *The Secret History*. Apparently, Reverend Fontaine was very fond of bear meat, for Byrd

describes at one point his "growling like a wildcat over a squirrel" as
he ate it, and at another, as they are leaving the Dan River region, he
says the chaplain's spirits are down, since they are leaving "the latitude
of fat bear." Whether Bearskin believed the tale he told Byrd about the
sexually charged powers of a bear-meat diet or was in turn spoofing
the white men (he shows himself several times to have a quick sense
of humor), Byrd passes the information along in mock seriousness. It
is very possible that bear meat, like oysters, was rumored by settlers
and Native Americans alike to increase sexual potency.

In a similar joking entry in *The Secret History,* dated 12 November,
Byrd says that the chaplain "of all worldly food conceives this [bear
meat] to be the best." Then he adds, "Though, in truth, 'tis too rich for
a single man and inclines the eater of it strongly to the flesh, insomuch
that whoever makes a supper of it will certainly dream of a woman or
the devil, or both" (*SH* 141).

1 NOVEMBER 1728

> By the negligence of one of the men in not hobbling his horse,
> he straggled so far that he could not be found. This stopped us
> all the morning long; yet, because our time should not be en-
> tirely lost, we endeavored to observe the latitude by twelve
> o'clock. Though our observation was not perfect by reason
> the wind blew a little too fresh, however, by such a one as we
> could make, we found ourselves in 36 degrees 20 minutes only.
> Notwithstanding our being thus delayed and the unevenness of
> the ground over which we were obliged to walk (for most of us
> now served in the infantry), we traveled no less than six miles.
> Though as merciful as we were to our poor beasts, another of
> 'em tired by the way and was left behind for the wolves and
> panthers to feast upon. . . .
>
> The chief discouragement at present from penetrating far into
> the wilderness is the trouble of carrying a load of provisions. I
> must own, famine is a frightful monster and for that reason to be
> guarded against as well as we can. But the common precautions
> against it are so burdensome that people cannot tarry long out

and go far enough from home to make any effectual discovery. The portable provisions I would furnish our foresters withal are glue broth and rockahominy: one contains the essence of bread, the other of meat (*H* 278–79).

"36 degrees 20 minutes only"

Byrd's calculation of his position must surely have been off, for this position would have put them some eleven and a half miles south of the line. The difficulty of making precise observations in 1728, before even the sextant was invented, makes the relative accuracy of nearly all Byrd's survey all the more remarkable.

"Glue broth and rockahominy"

As the travelers retraced the line, covering territory that was already familiar, there were fewer new sights to record. Consequently, Byrd began wandering in his writing. For the next several days his musings include recipes, the history of Indian warfare in the area, the kinds of pack animals best suited to such exploration, the power of lightning, the fertility and suitability of the land just south of the Dan for farming, the power of music to raise spirits, the practice of dancing to cure the bite of the European tarantula, and (of all things) ambergris—which he declares to be "the dung of the spermacetti whale."

Byrd breaks off these wandering thoughts and opinions from time to time to describe a particular plant or animal or to make some comment on the potential uses of the medicinal plants he finds.

The "glue broth and rockahominy" he describes are very close to what we would now call beef boullion and grits. He makes extreme claims for both as being able to nourish a traveler for months in the absence of available game. He also points out in several passages that the men survived the journey much better than their horses did, partly because the men could almost always find plenty to eat. Several of the horses, weakened by two months of hard work and inadequate food (canes are not, as Byrd noted, very good fodder for horses), had to be abandoned along the way.

2 NOVEMBER 1728

The heavens frowned this morning and threatened abundance of
rain, but our zeal for returning made us defy the weather and de-
camp a little before noon. Yet we had not advanced two miles
before a soaking shower made us glad to pitch our tent as fast as
we could. We chose for that purpose a rising ground a half mile
to the east of Matrimony Creek. This was the first and only time
we were catched in the rain during the whole expedition
(*H* 280–81).

East of Matrimony Creek

The site was directly south of the present town of Martinsville,
Virginia. It is an area of low but fairly steep hills and valleys, still
heavily wooded, lying between the Berry Hill Road (which becomes
North Carolina 770 below the line) and Virginia 87. Byrd was by now
out of the mountains, and the rising rivers were the only impediments
to the return home.

3 NOVEMBER 1728

On the way our unmerciful Indian killed no less than two brace
of deer and a large bear. We only primed the deer, being unwilling to be encumbered with their whole carcasses. The rest we
consigned to the wolves, which in return serenaded us great part
of the night. They are very clamorous in their banquets, which
we know is the way some other brutes have, in the extravagance
of their jollity and sprightliness, of expressing their thanks to
Providence.

We came to our old camp in sight of the river Irvin, whose
stream was swelled now near four foot with the rain that fell the
day before. This made it impracticable for us to ford it, nor
could we guess when the water would fall enough to let us go
over. This put our mathematical professor, who should have
set a better example, into the vapors, fearing he should be
obliged to take up his winter quarters in that doleful wilderness (*H* 283–84).

"We only primed the deer"

By "priming" the deer, Byrd meant taking only the choicest cuts. Ordinarily, these would include the long fillets running on either side of the spine. The fillets are easily and quickly removed, and they are tender and have a good flavor. Priming might also involve taking the hams, or the largest cuts of tender meat from the top and back of the hams. There would be plenty left for the wolves, as he suggests.

The remark about the wolves' "expressing their thanks to Providence" by howling is oddly reminiscent of Christopher Smart's later poem about his cat, Jeoffrey, who also "worships in his way." Byrd could not have read Smart's poem, since it was not written until 1759.

"Whose stream was swelled"

The Smith River (which Byrd called the Irvin) flows out of the mountains north and west of Martinsville. Sudden, heavy rains in the mountains will cause it to climb out of its banks very quickly when it reaches the lower ground along the Virginia/North Carolina border.

4 November 1728

By some stakes we had driven into the river yesterday, we perceived the water began to fall but fell so slowly that we found we must have patience a day or two longer.

One of the young fellows we had sent to bring up the tired horses entertained us in the evening with a remarkable adventure he had met with that day. He had straggled, it seems, from his company in a mist and made a cub of a year old betake itself to a tree. While he was new priming his piece with intent to fetch it down, the old gentlewoman appeared and, perceiving her heir apparent in distress, advanced open-mouthed to his relief. The man was so intent upon his game that she had approached very near to him before he perceived her. But finding his danger, he faced about upon the enemy, which immediately reared upon her posteriors and put herself in battle array. The man, admiring at the bear's assurance, endeavored to fire upon her, but by the dampness of the priming his gun did not go off.

He cocked it a second time and had the same misfortune. After
missing fire twice, he had the folly to punch the beast with the
muzzle of his piece; but Mother Bruin, being upon her guard,
seized the weapon with her paws and by main strength
wrenched it out of the fellow's hands. The man, being thus fairly
disarmed, thought himself no longer a match for the enemy and
therefore retreated as fast as his legs could carry him. The brute
naturally grew bolder upon the flight of her adversary and pursued him with all her speed. For some time it was doubtful
whether fear made one run faster or fury the other. But after an
even course of about fifty yards, the man had the mishap to
stumble over a stump and fell down at his full length. He now
would have sold his life a pennyworth; but the bear, apprehend-
ing there might be some trick in the fall, instantly halted and
looked with much attention on her prostrate foe. In the meanwhile, the man had with great presence of mind resolved to
make the bear believe he was dead by lying breathless on the
ground, in hopes that the beast would be too generous to kill
him over again. To carry on the farce, he acted the corpse for
some time without daring to raise his hed to see how near the
monster was to him. But in about two minutes, to his unspeakable comfort, he was raised from the dead by the barking of a
dog belonging to one of his companions, who came seasonably
to his rescue and drove the bear from pursuing the man to take
care of her cub, which she feared might now fall into a second
distress (*H* 280–86).

"Pursued him with all her speed"

The lucky hunter is identified in *The Secret History* as John Ellis. In
that account, written earlier, the bear is a little more hesitant about approaching Ellis, though determined to defend her cub. Once Ellis attempts to strike her with the gun and she disarms him, he takes immediately to his heels. The bear, "being grown more bold by the flight
of her adversary, immediately pursued." The chase lasts forty yards before Ellis falls. The rest of the story is pretty much as Byrd tells it in
the later version.

I add the earlier account because it seems to me to explain how Ellis was able to get as far as he did. There was apparently some hesitation on the bear's part until she perceived that he was indeed in flight. Despite what Byrd says about large bears being fairly slow, they are really very fast on their feet, easily capable of outrunning even the fastest human under any circumstances. I retold the story to an acquaintance who has spent a great deal more time around bears than I have and asked his opinion. His only comment was, "I reckon she didn't want him very bad."

Byrd can be excused for stretching things a very little here. It is the kind of story that begs for elaboration.

5 NOVEMBER 1728

At the distance of about six miles we passed Cascade Creek, and three miles farther we came upon the banks of the Dan, which we crossed with much difficulty, by reason the water was risen much higher than when we forded it before.

We continued our march as far as Lowland Creek, where we took up our lodging for the benefit of the canes and winter grass that grew upon the rich grounds thereabouts. On our way thither we had the misfortune to drop another horse, though he carried nothing the whole day but his saddle. We showed the same favor to most of our horses, for fear, if we did not do it, we should in a little time be turned into beasts of burden ourselves. Custom had now made traveling on foot so familiar that we were able to walk ten miles with pleasure. . . .

The Indians, who have no way of traveling but on the hoof, make nothing of going twenty-five miles a day and carrying their little necessaries on their backs, and sometimes a stout pack of skins into the bargain. And very often they laugh at the English, who can't stir to a next neighbor without a horse, and say that two legs are too much for such lazy people, who can't visit their next neighbor without six. For their parts, they were utter strangers to all our beasts of carriage before the slothful Europeans came amongst them. They had on no part of the American continent, or in any of the islands, either horses or camels, drome-

daries, or elephants to ease the legs of the original inhabitants or
to lighten their labor. Indeed, in South America, and particularly
in Chile, they have a useful animal called "paco." This creature
resembles a sheep pretty much, only in the length of the neck
and figure of the head it is more like a camel (*H* 286–88).

"A useful animal called 'paco'"

Byrd describes an alpaca *(Lama pacos),* a domesticated relative of
the llama, an animal he had almost certainly never seen, except in pic-
tures. Like other digressions on whales and tarantulas, this one is not
included in *The Secret History.* Musing later on the poor condition of
the horses on the trip, Byrd no doubt grew interested in the history of
"beasts of carriage" in the New World, did some reading, and added
these passages. The rest of the description he gives of the llama is quite
detailed and suggests that he had researched the topic before writing
about it.

This is, in fact, the procedure he follows throughout *The History.*
The Secret History is an amusing, gossipy, event-filled account of the
survey. *The History* is intended for a different audience, one less interested in the personalities of the travelers and more interested in
the strange lands through which they traveled and the natural wonders they saw along the way. Byrd's exposure to the scientific fact-
gathering of the Royal Society is evident all through the document.

6 November 1728

The difficulty of finding the horses among the tall canes made it
late before we decamped. We traversed very hilly ground but,
to make amends, it was pretty clear of underwood. We avoided
crossing the Dan twice by taking a compass round the bent of it.
There was no passing by the angle of the river without halting a
moment to entertain our eyes again with that charming prospect.
When that pleasure was over, we proceeded to Sable Creek and
encamped a little to the east of it. The river thereabouts had a
charming effect, its banks being adorned with green canes sixteen feet high, which make a spring all the year as well as plenty
of forage.

One of the men wounded an old buck that was gray with years and seemed by the reverend marks he bore upon him to confirm the current opinion of that animal's longevity. The smart of his wound made him not only turn upon the dogs but likewise pursue them to some distance with great fury. However he got away at last, though by the blood that issued from his wound he could not run far before he fell and without doubt made a comfortable repast for the wolves. . . .

All the land we traveled over this day and the day before, that is to say, from the river Irvin to Sable Creek, is exceedingly rich, both on the Virginia side of the line and that of Carolina . . . as fertile as the lands were said to be about Babylon, which yielded, if Herodotus tells us right, an increase of no less than two or three hundred for one. But this hath the advantage of being a higher, and consequently a much healthier, situation than that. So that a colony of one thousand families might, with the help of moderate industry, pass their time very happily there. Besides grazing and tillage, which would abundantly compensate their labor, they might plant vineyards upon the hills, in which situation the richest wines are always produced. They might also propagate white mulberry trees, which thrive exceedingly in this climate, in order to the feeding of silkworms and making of raw silk. They might too produce hemp, flax, and cotton in what quantity they pleased, not only for their own use but likewise for sale. Then they might raise very plentifully orchards both of peaches and apples, which contribute as much as any fruit to the luxury of life (*H* 289–90).

"As fertile as the lands were said to be about Babylon"

The territory Byrd describes so enthusiastically here is precisely the area to which he returned a few years later, securing some twenty thousand acres of it for himself. His intention was to import a group of Swiss colonists to work it for him, as he had decided that the Swiss and the Germans were better, more reliable workers than the Scots and Irish who were immigrating into parts of North Carolina. Accordingly, he made several serious efforts to attract Swiss or German settlers, but he had little success. Eventually the area was settled, but mainly by people of Scots-Irish descent. Wright has a fascinating account of Byrd's efforts on behalf of his "Land of Eden" in his introduction to *The Prose Works* (31–32).

Again, it is interesting to note the difference between this lavish description of the territory (it reads almost like a real-estate advertisement) and the paucity of description in *The Secret History.* Probably Byrd had already made up his mind about what he would do with his purchase by the time he wrote the second account. It goes on to commend the climate (warm and pleasant, but with enough cold weather every year to keep the snakes and troublesome insects in check), and to list other kinds of fruit crops that can or cannot be grown successfully in such a place.

The farmland in the area today is given over largely to small tobacco allotments, cattle and dairy farming, and small grains. Danville, just north of the line, became an important center for tobacco and for cotton textiles. Eden, south of the line, is mainly a farming community that historically depended on the trade in tobacco.

White mulberry trees

Both the white mulberry *(Morus alba)* and the somewhat larger red mulberry *(Morus rubra)* are found in the area. The latter, a native tree, is far more common than the former, which was imported from Asia and naturalized. Only the white mulberry is usually associated with silk making.

7 NOVEMBER 1728

After crossing the Dan, we made a march of eight miles over hills and dales as far as the next ford of that river. And now we were by practice become such very able footmen that we easily outwalked our horses and could have marched much farther, had it not been in pity to their weakness. . . .

Though practice will soon make a man of tolerable vigor an able footman, yet, as a help to bear fatigue, I used to chew a root of ginseng as I walked along. This kept up my spirits and made me trip away as nimbly in my half-jack boots as younger men could do in their shoes. This plant is in high esteem in China, where it sells for its weight in silver. . . . It grows also on the northern continent of America, near the mountains, but as sparingly as truth and public spirit. . . . It cheers the heart even of a man that has a bad wife and makes him look down with great composure on the crosses of the world. . . . It comforts the stomach and strengthens the bowels, preventing all colics and fluxes. . . . However, 'tis of little use in the feats of love, as a great prince once found, who, hearing of its invigorating quality, sent as far as China for some of it, though his ladies could not boast of any advantage thereby. . . .

The ticks are either deer ticks or those that annoy the cattle. The first kind are long and take a very strong gripe [*sic*], being most in remote woods above the inhabitants. The other are round and more gently insinuate themselves into the flesh, being in all places where cattle are frequent. Both these sorts are apt to be troublesome during the warm season, but have such an aversion to pennyroyal that they will attack no part that is rubbed with the juice of that fragrant vegetable. And a strong decoction of this is likewise the most effectual remedy against seed ticks, which bury themselves in your legs when they are so small you can hardly discern them without a microscope.

The horseflies are not only a great grievance to horses but likewise to those that ride them. . . . But dittany, which is to be had in the woods all the while those insects remain in vigor, is a sure defense against them. For this purpose, if you stick a bunch of it in the headstall of your bridle, they will be sure to keep a respectful distance. . . .

Bear's oil is used by the Indians as a general defense against every species of vermin. Among the rest, they say it keeps both bugs and mosquitoes from assaulting their persons, which would otherwise devour such uncleanly people. Yet bears' grease has no strong smell, as that plant which the Egyptians formerly used against mosquitoes, resembling our palma Christi, the juice of which smelt so disagreeably that the remedy was worse than the disease (*H* 293–94).

Ginseng

Byrd placed great confidence in the ginseng root for a variety of virtues, but he scoffs here at the idea of its effectiveness in "the feats of love." Ginseng grows in several areas along the line, and it is still greatly sought after for use in over-the-counter remedies and folk medicine. It is extremely popular in China, and about 95 percent of the American ginseng crop, both that produced by cultivation and that grown in the wild, is shipped each year to Asia. Federal guidelines regulate its sale and distribution in the United States, and it is illegal to harvest wild ginseng "before the red berries ripen and set seed in late summer or early autumn" (Foster and Duke 50). The root of the plant is fleshy and looks vaguely like the human form. As its Latin name, *Panax quinquefolius,* suggests, the leaves grow in clusters of five. Byrd does not report seeing any wild ginseng growing during his journey.

Pennyroyal

Pennyroyal *(Hedeoma pulegioides)*, a small, aromatic plant with blue flowers, grows in upland woods over much of the eastern United States. Radford et al. describe it as common in the Piedmont and mountains of the Carolinas, though rare in the coastal plain (*Manual* 916). The strong-smelling oil of the plant is still used as an insect repellent.

Dittany

American dittany *(Cunila origanoides)* is a member of the mint family. A a small perennial with a smell somewhat like that of oregano, it grows in dry woodlands over much of the eastern United States and is fairly common in the Piedmont of North Carolina and Virginia. Foster and Duke record its use, in the form of leaf tea, in treating colds, fevers, and headaches but do not mention it as an insect repellent.

It is interesting that Byrd spent as little time as he did in writing about the insects that must have plagued the surveyors. In earlier sections he mentions "that Carolina plague, mosquitoes," and here he discusses flies, ticks and "seed ticks" (which may have been small ticks but more likely, judging by the description, were chiggers). Perhaps the combination of dittany, pennyroyal, bears' oil, and whatever other concoctions the party may have had at its disposal proved at least minimally effective. Also, the style of dress customary in the eighteenth century would have protected the skin from some biting insects.

Bears' oil

Byrd has already mentioned the widespread use of bears' oil or fat by the Nottoways. (See his observations and the comments for 7 April, above.)

8 NOVEMBER 1728

As we had twice more to cross the Dan over two fords that lay no more than seven miles from each other, we judged the distance would not be much greater to go round the bent of it. Accordingly, we sent the Indian and two white men that way, who came up with us in the evening, after fetching a compass of twelve miles. They told us that about a mile from our last camp they passed a creek fortified with steep cliffs, which therefore gained the name of Cliff Creek. Near three miles beyond that they forded a second creek, and this was called Hix's Creek from one of the discoverers. Between these two creeks lies a level of exceeding rich land, full of large trees, and covered with black mold, as fruitful, if we believe them, as that which is yearly overflowed by the Nile. . . .

We catched a large terrapin in the river, which is one kind of turtle. The flesh of it is wholesome and good for consumptive people. It lays a great number of eggs, not larger but rounder than those of pigeons. These are soft but withal so tough that 'tis difficult to break them, yet are very sweet and invigorating, so that some wives recommend them earnestly to their husbands. One of the men, by an overstrain, had unhappily got a running of the reins, for which I gave him every morning a little sweet gum dissolved in water, with good success. This gum distills from a large tree, called the sweet gum tree, very common in Virginia, and is as healing in its virtue as balm of Gilead or the balsams of Tolú and of Peru. It is likewise a most agreeable perfume, very little inferior to ambergris (*H* 294–95).

"We catched a large terrapin in the river"

The "large terrapin" is probably a snapping turtle *(Chelydra serpentina),* which grows to considerable size and is edible. A large snapper may weigh as much as forty pounds. The eggs are, however, a great deal larger than pigeon eggs, being more nearly the size of Ping-Pong balls. If Byrd discovered the eggs inside the reptile, they might of course have been much smaller.

The sweet gum tree

This common tree *(Liquidambar styraciflua)* grows throughout the Piedmont area and often takes over old fields or areas that have recently been logged. It is, as Byrd notes, a large tree, growing to 125 feet or more, and it produces the familiar, prickly "balls"—actually the fruit of the tree, covered by a rough husk and projecting points. Since it grows faster than oaks, it is often one of the most common deciduous trees to reestablish itself in areas where the hardwoods have been cut out.

Traditionally, both the inner bark and the resin or "gum" of the tree have been used in folk medicine. The gum was often used (chewed or dissolved in water to make a tea, as Byrd described) as a treatment for diarrhea.

Having mentioned ambergris in his discussion of the virtues of the gum tree, Byrd spends much of the rest of this entry on a discussion of spermacetti and the perfume industry.

9 NOVEMBER 1728

> We reckoned ourselves now pretty well out of the latitude of bears, to the great grief of most of the company. There was still mast enough left in the woods to keep the bears from drawing so near to the inhabitants. They like not the neighborhood of merciless man till famine compels them to it. They are all black in this part of the world, and so is their dung, but it will make linen white, being tolerable good soap, without any preparation but only drying. These bears are of a moderate size, whereas within the polar circles they are white and much larger (*H* 296).

"The latitude of bears"

The entry for this date in *The Secret History* starts off, "Dr. Humdrum got up so early that it made him quite peevish, especially now we were out of the latitude of fat bear, with which he used to keep up his humor" (*SH* 138). Dr. Humdrum, of course, is the chaplain, Reverend Fontaine.

Most of the rest of this long entry is a digression on other bears, on music, and on the dance, "which cures those who in Italy are bit by the spider called the tarantula" (*H* 297). Byrd obviously takes stories of dancing to cure venomous spider bites with all seriousness. The entry ends with the observation that the company made it as far as Buffalo Creek.

10 NOVEMBER 1728

In a dearth of provisions our chaplain pronounced it lawful to make bold with the Sabbath and send a party out a-hunting. They fired the dry leaves in a ring of five miles' circumference, which, burning inwards, drove all the game to the center, where they were easily killed. 'Tis really a pitiful sight to see the extreme distress the poor deer are in when they find themselves surrounded with this circle of fire; they weep and groan like a human creature, yet can't move the compassion of those hardhearted people who are about to murder them. This unmerciful sport is called fire-hunting and is much practiced by the Indians and frontier inhabitants, who sometimes, in the eagerness of their diversion, are punished for their cruelty and are hurt by one another when they shoot across at the deer which are in the middle. . . .

Our hunters massacred two brace of deer after this unfair way, of which they brought us one brace whole and only the primings of the rest. . . .

One of the men, who had been an old Indian trader, brought me a stem of silk grass, which was about as big as my little finger. But, being so late in the year that the leaf was fallen off, I am not able to describe the plant. The Indians use it in all their little manufactures, twisting a thread of it that is prodigiously

strong. Of this they make their baskets and the aprons which
their women wear about their middles for decency's sake. These
are long enough to wrap quite round them and reach down to
their knees, with a fringe on the under part by way of ornament.
They put on this modest covering with so much art that the
most impertinent curiosity can't, in the negligentest of their mo-
tions or postures, make the least discovery. As this species of silk
grass is much stronger than hemp, I make no doubt but sailcloth
and cordage might be made of it with considerable improvement
(*H* 299–300).

Fire hunting

Byrd was unconcerned about many actions undertaken by his men
that we would now consider flagrant violations of game laws and af-
fronts to common decency. Among these are the killing and attempted
killing of very young deer and bear, not to mention the sheer number
of animals that were sometimes taken in one day. He shows outright
disapproval, though, at the thought of fire hunting. It was, as he points
out, a method commonly used among the Native Americans, but he was
disturbed by the practice, especially when his own party resorted to it.

Silk grass

This is not the spired-leaf silk grass *(Yucca filamentosa)* Byrd had
described earlier, when the company was still near Currituck Inlet, but
something else. It may be *Apocynum cannabinum,* sometimes called silk
grass or Indian hemp. The plant grows almost everywhere along the
line.

The style of the "apron," complete with fringe, that Byrd describes
here can be seen on the Indian women in John White's sixteenth-
century paintings of the inhabitants of Roanoke Island. According to
Thomas Harriot, though, those garments were made of deerskin.

11 NOVEMBER 1728

We had all been so refreshed by our day of rest that we decamped earlier than ordinary and passed the several fords of
Hyco River. . . . We took up our quarters upon Sugartree Creek,

in the same camp we had lain when we came up, and happened
to be entertained at supper with a rarity we had never had the
fortune to meet with before during the whole expedition.

A little wide of this creek, one of the men had the luck to
meet with a young buffalo of two years old. It was a bull which,
notwithstanding he was no older, was as big as an ordinary ox.
His legs were very thick and very short and his hoofs exceeding
broad. His back rose into a kind of bunch a little above the
shoulders, which I believe contributes not a little to that creature's enormous strength. His body is vastly deep from the
shoulders to the brisket, sometimes six feet in those that are full
grown. The portly figure of this animal is disgraced by a shabby
little tail, not above twelve inches long. This he cocks up on end
whenever he's in passion and, instead of lowing or bellowing,
grunts with no better grace than a hog. The hair growing on his
head and neck is long and shagged and so soft that it will spin
into thread not unlike mohair, which might be wove into a sort
of camlet. Some people have stockings knit of it that would have
served an Israelite during his forty years' march through the
wilderness. Its horns are short and strong, of which the Indians
make large spoons which they say will split and fall to pieces
whenever poison is put into them. Its color is a dirty brown and
its hide so thick that it is scarce penetrable. However, it makes
very spongy sole leather by the ordinary method of tanning,
though this fault might by good contrivance be mended.

As thick as this poor beast's hide was, a bullet made shift to
enter it and fetch him down. It was found all alone, which seldom buffaloes are. They usually range about in herds like other
cattle, and, though they differ something in figure, are certainly
of the same species. There are two reasons for this opinion: the
flesh of both has exactly the same taste and the mixed breed betwixt both, they say, will generate (*H* 300–301).

"A young buffalo"

For more on buffalo and their disappearance from the area, see the
comments under Byrd's entry for 3 October, above. Typically, Byrd

speculates on the potential usefulness of such an animal for the English, and he mentions that buffalo and cattle can interbreed, producing fertile offspring. It is interesting that a farmer along the Dan River,
just east of the site of Byrd's last crossing of the river and only a few
miles from Buffalo Creek, recently introduced a herd of beefalo (animals produced by crossing beef cattle with buffalo) onto his land. At
this writing the animals are still on the farm.

12 NOVEMBER 1728

> Before we marched this morning, every man took care to pack
> up some buffalo steaks in his wallet, besides what he crammed
> into his belly. When provisions were plenty, we always found it
> difficult to get out early, being too much embarrassed with a
> long-winded breakfast. However, by the strength of our beef,
> we made a shift to walk about twelve miles, crossing Bluewing
> and Tewahominy creeks. And because this last stream received
> its appellation from the disaster of a Tuscarora Indian, 'twill not
> be straggling much out of the way to say something of that par-
> ticular nation.
>
> These Indians were heretofore very numerous and powerful,
> making, within time of memory, at least a thousand fighting
> men. Their habitation before the war with Carolina was on the
> north branch of Neuse River, commonly called Connecta Creek,
> in a pleasant and fruitful country. But now the few that are left
> of that nation live on the north side of Moratuck, which is all
> that part of Roanoke below the great falls toward Albemarle
> Sound (*H* 302).

"A Tuscarora Indian"

Almost all the rest of this lengthy entry concerns the Tuscarora
tribe, which, after bearing lengthy grievances from the whites around
them, went to war in North Carolina in 1711. According to Theda
Perdue, the Indians, led by Chief Hancock, attacked settlements in Bath
County, killing about 120 English inhabitants before being finally sub-
dued by a combined force of North Carolinians, South Carolina mili-

tia, and 500 Catawba Indians. (See the discussion of Indian tribes in chapter 3.)

The Tuscaroras' first act of war against the colonists was the capture of two men, John Lawson and Baron Christopher de Graffenried, in September of 1711. Lawson was a surveyor and amateur naturalist like Byrd, and the two men met at least once—on 27 July 1711, in Williamsburg. Byrd recorded the meeting in his diary. Byrd had also read Lawson's *A New Voyage to Carolina,* and some of the comments and descriptions from that book found their way into *The History.* After the capture Baron de Graffenried was set free, but Lawson was executed by the Tuscaroras for some real or imagined affront. Byrd says that the Indians cut his throat; others versions of the story say that he was tortured to death by the method both he and Byrd described as common among the Indians—that is, by having pine splinters driven into his flesh and set afire.

Connecta Creek

This is now called Contentnea Creek. It was the site of a Tuscarora town and also the body of water along which John Lawson lived for a while.

13 NOVEMBER 1728

We pursued our journey with all diligence and forded Ohimpamony Creek about noon, and from thence proceeded to Yapatsco, which we could not cross without difficulty. The beavers had dammed up the water much higher than we found it at our going-up, so that we were obliged to lay a bridge over a part that was shallower than the rest to facilitate our passage. Beavers have more of instinct, that half brother of reason, than any other animal, especially in matters of self-preservation.

The flesh of the beaver is tough and dry, all but the tail, which, like the parrot's tongue, was one of the farfetched rarities with which Heliogabalus used to furnish his luxurious table. The fur of these creatures is very valuable, especially in the more northern countries, where it is longer and finer. This the Dutch have lately contrived to mix with their wool and weave into a sort of drugget that is not only warm but wonderfully light and soft. They also make gloves and stockings of it that keep out the cold almost as well as the fur itself and don't look quite so savage. . . .

We encamped on Massamony Creek, after a journey of more than eleven miles. Along the way we shot a fat doe and a wild turkey, which fed us all plentifully. And we have reason to say, by our own happy experience, that no man need to despair of his daily bread in the woods whose faith is but half so large as his stomach (*H* 304 – 6).

"Beavers have more of instinct"

Byrd offers lengthy commentary in this entry on the habits of beavers. Some of what he says is true, but a great deal is superstition — such as when he describes the "master beaver" chastising lazy members of his group by beating them "with the flat of his tail, wherewith he is able to give unmerciful strokes." Byrd relies for some of his information and misinformation on Pliny, Claudius Aelianus, and others, and he often passes along without comment their descriptions of animal behavior.

"The flesh of the beaver is tough and dry"

Actually, the flesh of beaver is rather oily. The meat is dark and coarse grained, but it is not dry. The meat of the tail has long been esteemed as a delicacy. Its texture is firm, and it has a high fat content.

Byrd has nothing to say about the beaver as table fare in *The Secret History,* and this particular passage in *The History* has the air of something he thought up much later and inserted for the benefit of his English readers.

Byrd's comment about the value of beaver furs when they are mixed with wool and woven "into a sort of drugget" merely hints at the widespread demand for beaver pelts in the eighteenth and the early nineteenth centuries, when beavers were trapped relentlessly for the fur-hat trade. Hats made of beaver fur had been in demand in Europe since the 1500s, and they became extremely popular items of fashion for gentlemen from the reign of Charles I (1625 – 42) up through the 1830s and 1840s. The hairs making up the thick underlayer of beaver fur have tiny barbs. When the furs are treated with an arsenic bath, pressed, and dried to make felt, the little barbs interlock. The result is a material that is both tight and supple and that will shed water and hold its shape through continued wettings and hard use. (The use of arsenic in treating the furs meant that hatters were exposed to arsenic fumes during the drying process. Continued exposure often resulted in slurred speech, gross motor difficulties, and severely impaired mental functioning, giving rise to the expression, "mad as a hatter.")

Beavers became extinct in most of Europe by the late sixteenth century, and soon thereafter they were close to extinction in Scandinavia and Russia. The American fur trade revived the interest in beaver hats, the demand for the hats continuing until almost the middle of the nineteenth century. Small wonder, then, that beavers were nearly extirpated over much of their range and have only recently become commonplace again in North Carolina and Virginia.

14 NOVEMBER 1728

Being at length happily arrived within twenty miles of the uppermost inhabitants, we dispatched two men who had the ablest horses to go before and get a beef killed and some bread baked to refresh their fellow travelers upon their arrival. They had likewise orders to hire an express to carry a letter to the Governor giving an account that we were all returned in safety. This was the more necessary because we had been so long absent that many now began to fear that we were by this time scalped or barbecued by the Indians.

We decamped with the rest of the people about ten o'clock and marched near twelve miles. In our way we crossed Nutbush Creek, and four miles farther we came upon a beautiful branch of Great Creek, where we took up our quarters. . . .

The Indian killed a fawn which, being upon its growth, was not fat but made amends by being tender. He also shot an otter, but our people were now better fed than to eat such coarse food. The truth of it is, the flesh of this creature has a rank fishy taste and for that reason might be a proper regale for the Samoyeds, who drink the Czar of Muscovy's health and toast their mistresses in a bumper of train oil. The Carthusians, to save their vow of eating no flesh, pronounce this amphibious animal to be a fish and feed upon it as such without wounding their consciences. The skin of the otter is very soft, and the Swedes make caps and socks of it, not only for the warmth but also because they fancy it strengthens the nerves and is good against all distempers of the brain. The otter is a great devourer of fish, which are its natural food, and whenever it betakes itself to a vegetable diet it is as some high-spirited wives obey their husbands, by pure necessity.

One of our people shot a large gray squirrel with a very bushy tail, a singular use of which our merry Indian discovered to us. He said whenever this little animal has occasion to cross a run of water, he launches a chip or piece of bark into the water on which he embarks and, holding his tail to the wind, sails over very safely. If this be true, 'tis probable men learnt at first the use of sails from these ingenious little animals, as the Hottentots learnt the physical use of most of their plants from the baboons (H 306–7).

Otter

Otters, like beavers, were subject to unregulated trapping in the nineteenth century, and their numbers declined precipitously. Today they are fairly numerous along the Dan and Roanoke Rivers as well as elsewhere in the Southeast. The "Carthusians" Byrd jokes about were a contemplative order founded by St. Bruno in the eleventh century. Interestingly, the entry for this day in *The Secret History* makes no mention of an otter, noting instead that one man "killed a raccoon, the flesh of which is like pork, but truly we were better fed than to eat it" (SH 142). Why Byrd later substituted an otter for the raccoon is matter for conjecture. Whatever the reason, the substitution allows him to digress on the nature and eating habits of otters.

"A large gray squirrel with a very bushy tail"

This comes straight out of Byrd's reading, probably in Pliny. It almost certainly was not a part of Native American lore about squirrels.

Byrd makes no mention of a squirrel in his entry for 14 November in *The Secret History.* Once again, the addition in *The History* seems more an occasion for an entertaining digression than a record of an actual observation.

15 NOVEMBER 1728

About three miles from our camp we passed Great Creek, and then, after traversing very barren grounds for five miles together, we crossed the trading path and soon after had the pleasure of reaching the uppermost inhabitant. This was a plantation belonging to Colonel Mumford, where our men almost burst themselves with potatoes and milk. Yet as great a curiosity as a house was to us foresters, yet still we chose to lie in the tent, as being much the cleanlier and sweeter lodging.

The trading path above-mentioned receives its name from being the route the traders take with their caravans when they go to traffic with the Catawbas and other southern Indians. The Catawbas live about 250 miles beyond Roanoke River, and yet our traders find their account in transporting goods from Virginia to trade with them at their own town.

The course from Roanoke to the Catawbas is laid down nearest southwest and lies through a fine country that is watered by several beautiful rivers. Those of the greatest note are: first, Tar River, which is the upper part of Pamptico, Flat River, Little River, and Eno River, all three branches of the Neuse. . . .

In Santee River, as in several others in Carolina, a smaller kind of alligator is frequently seen, which perfumes the water with a musky smell. They seldom exceed eight feet in these parts, whereas near the equinoctial they come up to twelve or fourteen. And the heat of the climate don't only make them bigger but more fierce and voracious. They watch the cattle there when they come to drink and cool themselves in the river; and because they are not able to drag them into the deep water, they make up by stratagem what they want in force. They swallow great stones, the weight of which, being added to their strength, enables them to tug a moderate cow under water and, as soon as

they have drowned her, discharge the stones out of their maw
and then feast upon the carcass. However, as fierce and as strong
as these monsters are, the Indians will surprise them napping as
they float upon the surface, get astride their necks, then whip a
short piece of wood like a truncheon into their jaws, and holding the ends with their two hands, hinder them from diving by
keeping their mouths open; and when they are almost spent,
they will make to the shore, where their riders knock them on
the head and eat them (*H* 307–10).

"The trading path above-mentioned"

The Virginia traders frequently traveled to the lands of the Catawbas, on the North Carolina–South Carolina border very near present-
day Rock Hill, in order to exchange guns, powder, shot, hatchets,
blankets, kettles, and other durable goods for skins. The trading route,
which is clearly illustrated in the map the surveyors drew of the 1728
expedition, crossed the Roanoke River at what is now the upper end
of Lake Gaston, not far below Kerr Dam. Today, Interstate 85 crosses
at almost exactly the same place, headed in the same direction, carrying traffic in a southwesterly direction (as Byrd says, the "course . . . is
laid down nearest southwest") toward Charlotte, Rock Hill, and the
traditional lands of the Catawba Indians.

"Several beautiful rivers"

The trading route (now Interstate 85) would cross the Tar just
north of present-day Durham, North Carolina. The river Byrd calls the
Pamptico is the Pamlico. He goes on to describe the fertile land lying
within the river drainages and to enumerate other rivers and creeks,
some of which have been renamed since his time. Byrd had never
seen most of this territory, but he relied on reports of other travelers,
among them his contemporary and fellow surveyor, John Lawson.
Years before Byrd had come home from England, his father, William
Byrd I, had already become the most successful Virginia entrepreneur
ever to establish commerce with the Indians. In setting up trade with
the Catawbas and the Cherokees, the elder Byrd's traders had passed
through some of the country Byrd describes here.

"A smaller kind of alligator"

The animal is the same, *Alligator mississippiensis,* whether it is found in the Carolinas or in Florida. Alligators grow only during the warm seasons, when they are active and feeding; therefore, they grow more quickly and tend to grow larger in hot climates. Nonetheless, they have been known to reach lengths far in excess of 8 feet in both Carolinas. According to Palmer and Braswell, the largest recorded from North Carolina was one killed illegally on the South River in Carteret County in 1981. Professional herpetologists from Raleigh recorded its length at just over 12.5 feet and its weight at 474 pounds (270–71).

The descriptions of alligators swallowing stones and of Indians catching alligators by riding their backs and placing sticks in their jaws are pure fiction. Byrd simply adapted a report he had read in Pliny about crocodiles on the Nile in Africa.

After commenting on the towns of the Catawbas, Byrd describes their present situation and reiterates their long-standing enmity with the Tuscaroras, an enmity that had cost them dearly in past years. He ends the digression by expressing disapproval of the way the English had treated the native inhabitants, bringing the destructive Tuscarora war on themselves: "The Indians opened the war by knocking most of those little tyrants on the head that dwelt amongst them under pretense of regulating their commerce, and from thence carried their resentment so far as to endanger both North and South Carolina" (*H* 311).

16 NOVEMBER 1728

We gave orders that the horses should pass Roanoke River at Moniseep Ford, while most of the baggage was transported in a canoe. We landed at the plantation of Cornelius Keith, where I beheld the wretchedest scene of poverty I had met with in this happy part of the world. . . .

I am sorry to say it, but idleness is the general character of the men in the southern parts of this colony as well as in North Carolina. The air is so mild and the soil so fruitful that very little labor is required to fill their bellies, especially where the woods afford such plenty of game. These advantages discharge the men from the necessity of killing themselves with work, and then for

the other article, of raiment, a very little of that will suffice in so
temperate a climate. . . .

From hence we moved forward to Colonel Mumford's other
plantation, under the care of Miles Riley, where by that gentleman's directions we were again supplied with many good things.
Here it was we discharged our worthy friend and fellow traveler,
Mr. Bearskin, who had so plentifully supplied us with provisions
during our long expedition. We rewarded him to his heart's content, so that he returned to his town loaden with riches and the
reputation of having been a great discoverer (*H* 311–12).

"Our worthy friend and fellow traveler, Mr. Bearskin"

In *The Secret History* Byrd spends more time on this description,
detailing (among other things) how Bearskin was paid. Byrd gave him
some money and "a pound of powder with shot in proportion." Also,
Bearskin kept the skins from all the deer he had killed along the journey, "and had them carried for him into the bargain" (*SH* 144).

17 NOVEMBER 1728

This being Sunday, we were seasonably put in mind how much
we were obliged to be thankful for our happy return to the inhabitants. Indeed, we had great reason to reflect with gratitude
on the signal mercies we had received. First, that we had day by
day been fed by the bountiful hand of Providence in the desolate
wilderness, insomuch that if any of our people wanted one single
meal during the whole expedition, it was entirely owing to their
own imprudent management. Secondly, that not one man of our
whole company had any violent distemper or bad accident befall
him, from one end of the line to the other. . . . And, lastly, that
many uncommon incidents have concurred to prosper our under-
taking. We had not only a dry spring before we went out, but the
preceding winter, and even a year or two before, had been much
drier than ordinary. This made not only the Dismal but likewise
most of the sunken grounds near the seaside just hard enough to
bear us, which otherwise had been quite unpassable. . . .

Besides all that, we were surprised by no Indian enemy, but all of us brought our scalps back safe upon our heads. This cruel method of scalping of enemies is practiced by all the savages in America and perhaps is not the least proof of their original from the northern inhabitants of Asia (*H* 312–13).

"This cruel method of scalping"

Byrd repeats himself in the treatise that follows on scalping; he covered the subject earlier in much the same way in the entry for 20 October, pointing out that the custom was practiced by "the ancient Scythians, . . . who carried about these hairy scalps as trophies of victory." Scalping was practiced by several of the North American tribes before the arrival of the white man, but the English and (to a lesser extent) the French actually made it more widespread. The practice of offering monetary rewards for Indian scalps, especially during the French and Indian War of 1755–63, did more than anything else to insure that it became a custom universal to all the tribes.

18 NOVEMBER 1728

We proceeded over a level road twelve miles as far as George Hix's plantation on the south side Meherrin River, our course being for the most part northeast. . . .

All the grandees of the Saponi nation did us the honor to repair hither to meet us, and our worthy friend and fellow traveler, Bearskin, appeared among the gravest of them in his robes of ceremony. Four young ladies of the first quality came with them, who had more the air of cleanliness than any copper-colored beauties I had ever seen; yet we resisted all their charms, notwithstanding the long fast we had kept from the sex and the bear diet we had been so long engaged in. . . .

The most uncommon circumstance in this Indian visit was that they all come on horseback, which was certainly intended for a piece of state, because the distance was but three miles and 'tis likely they had walked twice as far to catch their horses. The men rode more awkwardly than any Dutch sailor, and the ladies

bestrode their palfreys à la mode de France but were so bashful
about it that there was no persuading them to mount till they
were quite out of our sight (*H* 315–16).

"The men rode more awkwardly than any Dutch sailor"

Byrd had already commented on the Indians' lack of interest in using the horse or other draft animals. This is in sharp contrast to the
tribes of the West and Southwest, who had long since become expert
riders. The reference to the Saponi women riding their horses *à la mode
de France* means that they, like French women, sat astride their mounts
rather than riding sidesaddle.

Byrd's own comments about the difficulty of keeping horses well
fed and healthy on the journey may suggest why the Saponis and other
Virginia tribes at this time had relatively little use for the horse as a
draft animal or a means of transportation. Rountree points out that the
coastal Powhatan Indians "took little interest" in horses (27), and in
fact horses were not much used by any of the eastern tribes in the
eighteenth century.

Much of the rest of this fairly long entry is a digression on the history of the Saponi tribe.

19 November 1728

In the distance of five miles we forded Meherrin Creek, which
was very near as broad as the river. About eight miles farther we
came to Sturgeon Creek, so called from the dexterity an Occa-
neechi Indian showed there in catching one of those royal fish,
which was performed after the following manner: in the sum-
mertime 'tis no unusual thing for sturgeons to sleep on the surface of the water, and one of them, having wandered up into
this creek in the spring, was floating in that drowsy condition.
The Indian above-mentioned ran up to the neck into the creek a
little below the place where he discovered the fish, expecting
the stream would soon bring his game down to him. He judged
the matter right, and as soon as it came within his reach, he
whipped a running noose over its jowl. This waked the stur-

geon, which, being strong in its own element, darted immediately under water and dragged the Indian after him. The man made it a point of honor to keep his hold, which he did to the apparent danger of being drowned. Sometimes both the Indian and the fish disappeared for a quarter of a minute and then rose at some distance from where they dived. At this rate they continued flouncing about, sometimes above and sometimes under water, for a considerable time, till at last the hero suffocated his adversary and haled his body ashore in triumph (*H* 316–17).

Sturgeon Creek

There is a small town called Sturgeonville and a nearby creek called Sturgeon Creek in Brunswick County, Virginia, to the northwest of Byrd's location when he made this entry.

The Atlantic sturgeon *(Acipenser oxyrhynchus)* is an enormous fish that often enters freshwater rivers and streams to spawn. Sturgeons grow up to fourteen feet long and can weigh as much as eight hundred pounds. Overfishing, water pollution, and the presence of dams blocking their spawning routes have all contributed to a vast reduction in the numbers of Atlantic sturgeon anywhere in the Southeast. I have seen Atlantic sturgeons only rarely, and I have never seen any of the huge ones such as Byrd describes here. They are a protected species in both Virginia and North Carolina at this time.

Sturgeons are slow-moving bottom-feeders for the most part. They are covered with large scales like bony plates and have elongated snouts. It would be possible to place a noose over the snout, as Byrd says the Indian does in this account. Interestingly, he makes no mention at all of the fish-catching incident in *The Secret History,* saying only that the party crossed a body of water he called "Sturgeon Run." It is very likely that the story he tells here is second- or thirdhand and that he recalled it and wrote it down sometime after he wrote *The Secret History.* He does not say he witnessed the incident, though his details clearly intend to give that impression. He does mention that the incident occurred in the spring of the year, so he could not, at any rate, have seen it on this trip.

20 NOVEMBER 1728

In the morning colonel Bolling, who had been surveying in the neighborhood, and Mr. Walker, who dwelt not far off, came to visit us; and the last of these worthy gentlemen, fearing that our drinking so much water might incline us to pleurisies, brought us a kind supply both of wine and cider. . . .

We crossed Nottoway River not far from our landlord's house, where it seemed to be about twenty-five yards over. This river divides the county of Prince George from that of Brunswick. We had not gone eight miles farther before our eyes were blessed with the sight of Sapony Chapel, which was the first house of prayer we had seen for more than two calendar months. About three miles beyond that, we passed over Sapony Creek, where one of those that guarded the baggage killed a polecat, upon which he made a comfortable repast. Those of his company were so squeamish they could not be persuaded at first to taste, as they said, of so unsavory an animal; but seeing the man smack his lips with more pleasure than usual, they ventured at last to be of his mess, and instead of finding the flesh rank and high tasted they owned it to be the sweetest morsel they had ever eat in their lives. The ill savor of this little beast lies altogether in its urine, which nature had made so detestably ill scented on purpose to furnish a helpless creature with something to defend itself. For as some brutes have horns and hoofs, and others are armed with claws, teeth, and tusks for their defense; and as some spit a sort of poison at their adversaries, like the paco; and others dart quills at their pursuers, like the porcupine; and as some have no weapons to help themselves but their tongues, and others none but their tales; so the poor polecat's safety lies altogether in the irresistible stench of its water, insomuch that when it finds itself in danger from an enemy it moistens its bushy tail plentifully with this liquid ammunition and then, with great fury, sprinkles it like a shower of rain full into the eyes of its assailant, by which it gains time to make its escape. Nor is the polecat the only animal that defends itself by a stink. At the Cape of Good Hope is a little beast called a "stinker," as big as a fox and

shaped like a ferret, which, being pursued, has no way to save itself but by farting and sqittering, and then such a stench ensues
that none of its pursuers can possibly stand it (*H* 318–19).

"Killed a polecat"

This is another incident that is not described at all in *The Secret
History*. Probably, since the skunk *(Mephitis mephitis)* was (and still is,
for that matter) a common small animal in both states, Byrd thought
it not worth a reference until he began putting together the draft of
The History, at which time he probably considered the interest Europeans might have in the account of such an animal.

Skunks do not, of course, fling their urine on would-be attackers.
The scent comes from two highly developed musk glands under the
base of the tail, near the anus. The popular belief that the animal dips
its tail into the musk (or, as Byrd would have it, into the urine) and
then flings the smell on its enemies with a shake of the tail probably
comes from the animal's warning displays. It will often stamp its feet
and raise its tail when alarmed before actually spraying. The spray can
carry a distance of ten feet or more.

One question immediately occurs to almost everyone who reads
this entry: "How did the man skin the skunk and prepare it for cooking without getting covered with the odor?" (I have not yet found anyone curious about the actual taste of the animal.) Trappers and others
have assured me that a skunk that has not been alarmed and has not
yet begun to spray before it dies will not release its odor after death.
In theory at least, it may then be skinned very carefully.

22 NOVEMBER 1728

A little before noon we all took leave and dispersed to our several habitations, where we were so happy as to find all our families well. This crowned all our other blessings and made our
journey as prosperous as it had been painful. Thus ended our
second expedition, in which we extended the line within the
shadow of the Cherokee mountains, where we were obliged to
set up our pillars, like Hercules, and return home. We had now,
upon the whole, been out about sixteen weeks, including going

and returning, and had traveled at least six hundred miles, and no small part of that distance on foot. Below, toward the seaside, our course lay through marshes, swamps, and great waters; and above, over steep hills, craggy rocks, and thickets, hardly penetrable. Notwithstanding this variety of hardship, we may say without vanity that we faithfully obeyed the king's orders and performed the business effectually in which we had the honor to be employed. Nor can we by any means reproach ourselves of having put the Crown to any exorbitant expense in this difficult affair, the whole charge, from beginning to end, amounting to no more than £1,000. But let no one concerned in this painful expedition complain of the scantiness of his pay so long as His Majesty has been graciously pleased to add to our reward the honor of his royal approbation and to declare, notwithstanding the desertion of the Carolina commissioners, that the line by us run shall hereafter stand as the true boundary betwixt the governments of Virginia and North Carolina (*H* 320–21).

The concluding entry in *The Secret History* has less of a flourish and is more matter-of-fact, detailing the arrival of family members, the directions various members of the party took on their ways home, and reports of illness among the families left behind. (Byrd's own son had been grievously ill during his absence.) It ends on a note of thanks: "My neighbors had been kind to my wife when she was threatened with the loss of her son and heir. Their assistance was kind as well as seasonable, when her child was threatened with fatal symptoms and her husband upon a long journey exposed to great variety of perils. Thus, surrounded with the most fearful apprehensions, Heaven was pleased to support her spirits and bring back her child from the grave and her husband from the mountains, for which blessings may we be all sincerely thankful" (*SH* 149).

Byrd's enumeration of the kinds of topography the company traveled through ("marshes, swamps, and great waters; . . . steep hills, craggy rocks, and thickets") in running the line from the sea to "within the shadow of the Cherokee mountains" is a fair description of the varied landscape of both North Carolina and Virginia. But how that land-scape has changed!

It is now possible to drive almost anywhere along Byrd's line, com-ing within a few miles of his actual survey. In fact, along the whole 241-mile stretch from the Atlantic Ocean to the mountains south of Stuart, Virginia, there are only a few spots more than 5 miles in any di-rection from a paved road. (All of these are near or south of the Great Dismal Swamp.)

Byrd's line is cut by two major interstates (Interstates 85 and 95) and a host of smaller state and federal highways. Little farming towns and villages (Virgilina, Milton, Corapeake, Norlina) come within yards of the path he took—or rather made for himself—in 1728. U.S. 158 runs east and west, paralleling Byrd's line on the south for 200 miles and coming within 10 miles of the border for much of its length. U.S. 58 in Virginia parallels the line to the north.

The area William Byrd knew only as "the great falls of the Roa-noke" is now the city of Roanoke Rapids, North Carolina. The city of Richmond would be laid out in a survey conducted partly by Byrd him-self and partly by his indefatigable surveyor and companion, William Mayo ("Astrolabe" of *The Secret History*), nine years later, in 1737. The city of Norfolk, just north of the line on the Elizabeth River, Byrd de-scribed in 1728 as a promising little town having "all the advantages of situation requisite for trade and navigation." Norfolk is now home to almost a quarter of a million people, and the metropolitan area of which Norfolk is a part has a total population of over one and a half million, making it the twenty-eighth most populous metropolitan area in the United States.

In the early eighteenth century the most important town in the colony of North Carolina was Edenton. Today Edenton is a beautiful, picturesque little town with a rich sense of history, but its impor-tance as a port and a center of government vanished long ago. The body of water Byrd named Nutbush Creek is now part of a huge, man-made reservoir as wide as—and much deeper than—the sound called Back Bay, which he and his men picked their way across in the early spring of 1728.

Byrd several times expressed the hope that more settlers would populate "His Majesty's colony" (meaning Virginia). More did, and they populated the Colony of North Carolina as well. Today, their descendants and others who have immigrated there make the combined populations of both states around 15 million people. They built cities and dams and farms, changing the land in ways Byrd could only have imagined in dreams.

And yet, for all that, much has remained. The great chestnut trees are gone, of course, and so are the panthers and the buffalo and elk. But there are places along the line where nature looks much the same as it did nearly 275 years ago. If he were back today, Byrd could still find the medicinal herbs and useful plants he described in *The History*. The Dismal Swamp as a whole is about as strange and forbidding now as it was then, except that now one can take a boardwalk path into one edge of it for the purpose of studying its flora and fauna. The turkeys and squirrels and wildcats, along with the blue-winged teal and most of the other animals and birds he mentioned, are still around in considerable numbers. The deer are more numerous now than they were when he drew the line.

Byrd crossed the Dan River just over a mile behind the place where I sit now, roughly in the direction I face as I type this sentence. Perhaps I will walk down to the river later. I will have to cross one small paved road, but most of the walk will be through woods—some of them planted stands of loblolly pine, which Byrd never mentioned, but also groves of white oak and red oak and hickory (all trees he describes in the area). There will be canes growing close to the river's edge. On the way I will probably see a deer or a turkey at least. Twice I have seen wildcats here, and once in a very great while it is possible to see the track of a fat bear. I think William Byrd would be pleased at that.

Works Cited

Audubon, John James. "Pitting of Wolves." In *Hunting in the Old South: Original Narratives of the Hunters,* edited by Clarence Ghodes, 80–86. Baton Rouge: Louisiana University Press, 1967.

Beane, Jeff. "Longleaf Pine Forests." *Wildlife in North Carolina* 64, no. 2 (2000): 28–31.

Byrd, William. *The Prose Works of William Byrd of Westover.* Edited by Louis B. Wright. Cambridge: The Belknap Press of Harvard University Press, 1966.

"Chestnut Trees Replanted in N.C. Mountains." *North Carolina Sportsman* 8, no. 7 (2001): 32–33.

Fernald, Merritt Lyndon. *Gray's Manual of Botany,* 8th ed. New York: American Book Company, 1950.

Foster, Stephen, and James A. Duke. *A Field Guide to Medicinal Plants: Eastern and Central North America.* Boston: Houghton Miflin, 1990.

Harriot, Thomas. *A Briefe and True Report of the New Found Land of Virginia: The Complete 1590 Edition.* New York: Dover Publications, 1972.

Harvill, A. M., Jr. *Spring Flora of Virginia.* Parsons, W.Va.: McCain Printing Company, 1972.

Kuser, John E., and George Zimmerman. "Restoring Atlantic White Cedar Swamps: A Review of Techniques for Propagation and Establishment." *Tree Planter's Notes* 49, no. 3 (1995): 78–85.

McCary, Ben C. *Indians in Seventeenth-Century Virginia.* Charlottesville: University Press of Virginia, 1957.

Marambaud, Pierre. *William Byrd of Westover: 1674–1744.* Charlottesville: University Press of Virginia, 1971.

Martof, Bernard, et al. *Amphibians and Reptiles of the Carolinas and Virginia.* Chapel Hill: University of North Carolina Press, 1980.

Millspaugh, Charles F. *American Medicinal Plants: An Illustrated and Descriptive Guide.* New York: Dover Publications, 1974.

Nickens, Edward. "A Brief Glance Backwards." *Wildlife In North Carolina* 64, no. 1 (2000): 14–17.

O'Brien, Timothy G., and Phillip D. Doerr. "Night Count Surveys for Alligators in Coastal Counties of North Carolina." *Journal of Herpetology* 20, no. 3 (1986): 444–48.

Palmer, William M., and Alvin L. Braswell. *Reptiles of North Carolina.* Chapel Hill: University of North Carolina Press, 1995.

Perdue, Theda. *Native Carolinians: The Indians of North Carolina.* Raleigh: North Carolina Department of Cultural Resources, 1991.

Radford, Albert E., et al. *Atlas of the Vascular Flora of the Carolinas.* Chapel Hill: The North Carolina Agriculture Experiment Station, 1964.

——. *Guide to the Vascular Flora of the Carolinas.* Chapel Hill: University of North Carolina Press, 1968.

——. *Manual of the Vascular Flora of the Carolinas.* Chapel Hill: University of North Carolina Press, 1968.

Rountree, Helen. *The Powhatan Indians of Virginia: Their Traditional Culture.* Norman: University of Oklahoma Press, 1988.

Ryden, Hope. *Lily Pond: Four Years with a Family of Beavers.* New York: William Morrow, 1989.

Savage, Henry, Jr. *Lost Heritage.* New York: William Morrow, 1970.

Simpson, Bland. *The Great Dismal: A Swamp Memoir.* New York: Henry Holt, 1993.

Wright, Louis B. "Introduction: William Byrd as a Man of Letters." In *The Prose Works of William Byrd of Westover,* edited by Louis B. Wright. Cambridge: The Belknap Press of Harvard University Press, 1966.

Selected Index